STRANGERS ON A HILL

CONGRESS AND THE COURT

CONGRESS AND THE COURT

ROSS K. BAKER

W. W. Norton & Company

New York ■ London

W. W. Norton & Company has been independent since its founding in 1923, when William Warder Norton and Mary D. Herter Norton first published lectures delivered at the People's Institute, the adult education division of New York City's Cooper Union. The Nortons soon expanded their program beyond the Institute, publishing books by celebrated academics from America and abroad. By mid-century, the two major pillars of Norton's publishing program—trade books and college texts—were firmly established. In the 1950s, the Norton family transferred control of the company to its employees, and today—with a staff of four hundred and a comparable number of trade, college, and professional titles published each year—W. W. Norton & Company stands as the largest and oldest publishing house owned wholly by its employees.

The text of this book is composed in ITC Galliard.
with the display set in Berthold City.
Composition by MidAtlantic Books & Journals, Inc.
Manufacturing by Victor Graphics, Inc.
Book design by Lissi Sigillo.
Production manager: Benjamin Reynolds.

ISBN 10: 0-393-97856-7 (pbk.)
ISBN 13: 978-0-393-97856-8 (pbk.)

W. W. Norton & Company, Inc., 500 Fifth Avenue, New York, N.Y. 10110-0017
www.wwnorton.com
W. W. Norton & Company Ltd., Castle House, 75/76 Wells Street, London W1T 3QT
1 2 3 4 5 6 7 8 9 0

To Ellen: for her boundless love

C O N T E N T S

Acknowledgments

Throughout my career, I have depended heavily on the assistance of others in writing the books that I have produced. This book is no exception. People have given unstintingly of their time to answer questions on matters of which I knew little, especially when it came to explaining the arcane world of constitutional law and the equally recondite legislative process. Rarely did one interview suffice. I requested and received call-back privileges which, I confess, I often abused. To those people whose time I consumed with questions that someone with a more prehensile mind might have grasped the first time around, I offer both my sincerest apologies and most heartfelt thanks.

At the top of my list is former representative Steven Solarz, who patiently answered my questions and then thoughtfully directed me to another important source of information, attorney Nathan Lewin of Washington DC. Also at the top of the list of generous interviewees are Bruce Cohen, Chief Minority Counsel of the Senate Judiciary Committee, and David Lachmann, Minority Professional Staff Member of the House Judiciary Committee, a man with an encyclopedic knowledge of the history of free exercise legislation in the House of Representatives.

Two distinguished law professors who found themselves on opposite sides of the free exercise issue deserve to be singled out for praise—Professor Marci Hamilton of the Cardozo School of Law of Yeshiva University in New York and Professor Douglas Laycock of the University of Texas Law School.

At various times I needed to call on one of the top legal journalists in the country, Tony Mauro, Supreme Court Correspondent for *The American Lawyer*. Although Tony is not a lawyer, I would feel more comfortable getting legal advice from him than from many who have the union card. At an early stage of this project, I was fortunate to be able to draw upon an old friendship, with Richard Moe, president of the National Trust for Historic Preservation. He got me off to a good start.

In the course of my research into the case of *Sherbert v. Verner*, I had the good fortune to be assisted by the staff of the public library of Spartanburg, South Carolina. They in turn introduced me to Betsy Wakefield Teter of the Hub City Writers Project of Spartanburg, the editor of the splendid documentary history of the textile industry in Spartanburg, *Textile Town*.

In the chapter dealing with *Employment Division v. Smith*, I relied very heavily on the work of a former student, now a distinguished academic, Carolyn Nestor Long, Professor of Political Science at Washington State University and author of the definitive work on the case, *Religious Freedom and Indian Rights*. Another former student turned academic who assisted me at a critical time in the preparation of the manuscript is Professor Judithanne Scourfield McLauchlan of the University of South Florida, who has written the definitive work on *amicus curiae* briefs by members of Congress. My thanks also go to Professor Susan P. Fino of Wayne State University for help in preparing the proofs.

I owe much to my brief but fruitful association with the people of Boerne, Texas, the beautiful little Hill Country town whose community controversy gave us the landmark case of *Boerne v. Flores*. Special thanks are owed to Rev. Tony Cummins, pastor of St. Peter the Apostle Church, which was at the eye of the storm. Prominent on the other side of the controversy was Patrick Heath, mayor of the City of Boerne. Two other worthy opponents in the Boerne case were architect Greg Davis, who was responsible for the design for the enlargement of the church, and "Dub" Smothers, who not only led the opposition but provided a documentary record of the dispute as it unfolded. Dub gave unselfishly of his time by showing me around Boerne and San Antonio.

Finally, I had access to an organization that was matchless for the depth of its resources and the ability of its personnel, the Library of the United States Senate. My personal thanks go to Senate librarian C. Gregory Harness and his staff, especially Nancy Kervin, Senior Research Librarian.

It was during my 2004 sabbatical in the US Senate office of Senator Patrick J. Leahy that I was able to avail myself of the Senate library and the staff of the Judiciary Committee, including someone I met quite fortuitously, Lisa Graves, who was then serving as Chief Nominations Counsel for the Judiciary Committee and is now Senior Counsel for Legislative Strategy for the American Civil Liberties Union. Like a benevolent spirit, Lisa appeared at the latter stage of my research and provided me with some novel and useful perspectives.

I would also like to thank the remarkable members of Senator Leahy's personal office, especially his able and modest Chief of Staff, Luke Albee, now with the firm of Richetti, Inc., in Washington DC. My host Senator Leahy also deserves my thanks and the thanks of all friends of civil liberties for being the vigilant guardian of the rights of Americans at a time when some regard them only as necessarily evils.

Finally, I would like to thank my editor at W. W. Norton & Company, Steve Dunn, for his patience and forbearance with a manuscript that should probably have been on his desk months before it arrived. He and Roby Harrington, director of Norton's college division, have always been my steadfast friends. I am also indebted to Aaron Javsicas and Mikael Awake of Norton for their keen editorial eyes.

Introduction

On Sunday March 20, 2005, Palm Sunday, members of the US House of Representatives were called back to Washington from their Easter recess to vote on an unusual piece of legislation. What made it unusual was that it affected a single person—a forty-one-year-old brain-damaged woman named Terri Schiavo, who lay in a hospice in Pinellas Park, Florida. The bill granted to Terri Schiavo's parents the right to appeal to the federal courts in the hope that they would grant them the satisfaction denied them by the courts of the state of Florida. They sought the right to insert into their daughter a feeding tube that had been removed by direction of her husband, who wished to allow his wife to die. Without the reinsertion of the tube, Terri Schiavo would survive for perhaps two weeks before she died from dehydration.

Fifteen years earlier, in February 1990, Schiavo had suffered a heart attack that left her with what appeared to be irreversible brain damage. Her husband, Michael, became her legal guardian and tended to her for the next ten years. But in February 2000, Michael Schiavo appealed to a Florida state court to have his wife's feeding tube removed so that she could be allowed to die.

A series of battles in Florida courts and appeals to federal courts ensued. The courts consistently determined that Terri Schiavo wished not to be kept alive in such a reduced state of existence. The tube was removed. Subsequently, the state legislature of Florida passed a bill called "Terri's Law" that empowered Governor Jeb Bush to intervene in the case. He intervened, ordering the tube reinserted, but in September 2004, the Florida State Supreme Court declared that "Terri's Law" violated the Florida constitution. Governor Bush requested a hearing by the US Supreme Court, but the court declined to hear the case.

Once all remedies within the state of Florida were exhausted and the US Supreme Court declined a hearing, a Florida lawyer representing Governor Bush turned to Congress. He contacted Rep. Dave Weldon, a Republican who is also a physician, and asked that Congress grant Terri Schiavo's parents the right to appeal the case to the federal courts because congressional action was necessary to obtain a legal remedy known as an injunction. This would not have been available to them without an act of Congress, which has the power, under Article III of the Constitution, to determine the kinds of cases that federal courts can hear. Weldon secured the support of two influential Republicans in Congress—Bill Frist, the Republican Majority Leader in the Senate, also a medical doctor, and Tom DeLay, the Republican Majority Leader in the House. Weldon worked with the National Right to Life Committee to sponsor a bill granting to certain categories of incapacitated patients the right to appeal to federal courts.[1]

The US Senate passed a narrower bill granting only to the parents of Terri Schiavo the right to have their case heard in the federal courts. Accepting the Senate's version, the House, after a heated debate on March 20–21, passed the narrower Senate bill by a vote of 203 to 58, with 174 members not voting. The president, who was on vacation at his ranch in Crawford, Texas, flew back to Washington to sign the bill.

In the next ten days, the mother, father, sister, and brother of Terri Schiavo attempted once more to get a court to order the feeding tube reinserted. This time, the request was made to the US District Court for the Middle District of Florida, which turned down the Schiavos. The family then petitioned the US Court of Appeals for the Eleventh Circuit, which sits in Atlanta, Georgia, for an expedited hearing. It was the fourth time that this court had considered the case.

On March 30, 2005, a majority of the court voted to deny the emergency petition. The order, written by Chief Judge J. L. Edmondson, was a curt one-sentence denial. However, one of Edmondson's colleagues, Judge Stanley Birch, wrote a lengthy opinion concurring with Edmondson, in which he held that the bill passed by Congress was unconstitutional on the grounds that it dictated to the federal court the manner in which it was to conduct its review of the case. He wrote:

> In short, certain provisions of . . . the Act attempt to direct what particular steps are to be taken in the progress of a judicial inquiry. Because this is violative of the principles of separation of powers enshrined in our Constitution, they are unconstitutional.[2]

Judge Birch also used the occasion to deliver a lecture on constitutional law to Congress. He wrote:

> In resolving the Schiavo controversy, it is my judgment that, despite sincere and altruistic motivation, the legislative and executive branches of our government have acted in a manner demonstrably at odds with our Founding Fathers' blueprint for the governance of a free people—our Constitution. Since I have sworn, as they have, to uphold and defend that Covenant, I must respectfully concur in the denial of the request for rehearing . . . I conclude that Pub. L. 109-3 ("the Act") is unconstitutional. . . .[3]

The court's decision set off a flurry of angry comments from members of Congress. Rep. Tom Feeney (R-FL) denounced "the imperial judiciary." The previous week he had said, "The minute they put on those robes some of them become arrogant, supremacist ideologues who substitute their own biases and prejudices for representative government."[4]

In an even more menacing tone, Rep. Tom DeLay, the Republican Majority Leader in the House, warned, "The time will come for the men responsible for this to answer for their behavior, but not today." He accused the judges of having "thumbed their nose at Congress and the president" and hinted at the possibility that he might seek the impeachment of the judges who declined to hear the Schiavo appeal.[5]

On Thursday, March 31, 2005, Terri Schiavo died, but her death did not silence the debate over the moral implications of her husband's decision and the political consequences of Congress's decision to intervene in the case.

The Schiavo case, occurring as it did in the aftermath of the 2004 presidential election and a period of stark polarization between Democrats and Republicans in Congress,[6] appeared, on the face of it, to be a continuation of the culture wars, with social conservatives exploiting the Schiavo family's efforts to keep Terri alive for their own political purposes. Antiabortion groups such as the National Right to Life Committee had urged the Florida legislature and Congress to act on the family's behalf and paid their legal fees. While many Democrats in Congress stepped aside and let the Republican majorities in both houses pass the bill, what opposition there was came almost exclusively from Democrats. Of the fifty-eight House members who opposed the bill, only four were Republicans. Was the battle over whether Terri Schiavo would live or die just one more example of the war over moral values, such as abortion rights, same-sex marriage, the display of the Ten Commandments in public places, or teaching "intelligent design" in schools along with Darwin's theory of evolution?

There is something more here, however. What is interesting about the Schiavo case is what it tells us about the two centuries of struggle between the US Congress and the federal courts, a struggle rooted in one of the bedrock principles of American democracy—the separation of powers. Because of this principle, our government is divided into three branches: the legislative, the executive, and the judicial. In theory, no branch is permitted to infringe upon the powers granted to another branch. Thus, the anger of members of Congress at the courts for not granting a hearing to Terry Schiavo's family was directed not solely against a decision with which they disagreed on moral grounds; some regarded the decision as a usurpation by the courts of their policymaking functions. Likewise, the opinion by Judge Birch, one of the most conservative members of the Eleventh Judicial Circuit, was less a defense of the determination by Michael Schiavo that his wife's feeding tube be removed than a rebuke to Congress for presuming to instruct a court how to conduct its business.

It is the goal of this book to direct our attention to this basic contest between Congress and the courts. This contest is entirely normal and generally tends to promote a healthy democracy. As James Madison wrote:

> . . . [The] great security against a gradual concentration of the several powers in the same department, consists in giving to those who administer each department, the necessary means, and personal motives to resist encroachment of the others. . . . Ambition must be made to counteract ambition. The interest of the man must be connected with the constitutional rights of the place.[7]

One common arena for this contest is the realm of religion and morals; religious and moral issues will figure prominently in this book. The struggle can be easily be viewed as one of conflicting political ideologies. While not dismissing the ideological dimension, this book is primarily concerned with examining the complex interplay of constitutionally ordained tensions and personal factors that attach to the roles of judge and member of Congress.

Beginning in Chapter 3, we will examine the principle of separation of powers through the lens of a single issue—tensions between Congress and the federal courts over the proper interpretation of one of the key passages in the First Amendment of the Bill of Rights, the "Free Exercise Clause," which states that "Congress shall make no law respecting the establishment of religion, or prohibiting the free exercise thereof."

We will trace the disputatious history of this deceptively straightforward clause from its first airing in the nineteenth century in a case about the practice of polygamy to current disputes over religious practices within America's prisons, land use disputes involving churches, and others.

All these cases involve conflict between the United States Congress (the legislative branch of our national government) and the United States federal courts (the judicial branch), headed by the Supreme Court. The members of both of these bodies swear an oath upon taking office to uphold the Constitution. In practice, however, what it means to uphold the Constitution is often open to debate. On this issue the perspectives of a popularly elected legislator with an obvious desire to be a popularly re-elected legislator and that of a judge who, after Senate confirmation, serves for life, are distinct and often even antagonistic.

Making law and interpreting law are likewise different. Even if interpretation of the law were the only duty of the Supreme Court, the relationship between the Court and Congress would not necessarily be placid. But more than 200 years ago, a decision was handed down that asserted the Supreme Court's power of *judicial review*, and thereby made the relationship between the federal courts and Congress far more adversarial. It is one thing for a court to divine the correct meaning of a law passed by Congress. It is quite another for a court to challenge the very validity of a law, the power that judicial review provides.

It is to this momentous first decision that we will turn in Chapter 1. *Marbury v. Madison*, which was decided in 1803, is the logical place for us to start because that case established the Supreme Court's power of judicial review. We will examine the case and the precedent it established.

In Chapter 2, we encounter the first judicial examinations of the First Amendment's free exercise clause. We see how that clause, which during the nineteenth century applied only to actions by the federal government, came to be applied to the states. In that chapter we will also learn about the very strict standard imposed in 1963 by the Supreme Court on state actions that infringe on religious liberty.

In Chapter 3, we see a limitation on free exercise of religion and a reinforcement of another free exercise. The obligation of an employer to contribute to Social Security for his employees and the ability of an officer of the US military to get his service to bend its stringent dress code to accommodate his religious practice give us some sense of the variety of forms that we find in free exercise cases. More important for our purposes, the latter case involves the first modern instance of a direct confrontation between the Supreme Court and Congress over a matter on which the Constitution speaks with unmistakable clarity.

In Chapter 4, we see how the Supreme Court, in a case from the state of Oregon, substantially reduced the lofty standard that states must meet before moving to curtail a religious practice. The retreat was so dramatic that interest groups representing religious organizations besieged Congress for corrective legislation.

In Chapter 5 we see that Congress hastened to comply with these demands, passing the Religious Freedom Restoration Act. This action set up a direct conflict between Congress and the Court over which branch of the federal government should have the final word on the meaning of the free exercise clause.

Round two of the conflict is presented in Chapter 6. Congress, having acted to restore the most formidable barrier to state limits on religious practice, was confronted by the Supreme Court in a Texas case involving the seemingly prosaic issue of land use policy. What makes the case constitutionally significant is that the land in question was the property of a church. Congress's elaborately constructed Religious Freedom Restoration Act was declared invalid by the Court.

In Chapter 7, we see Congress striking back with yet another effort to prevent states from limiting religious practice. This time, with the Religious Land Use and Institutionalized Person Act of 2000 (RLUIPA), Congress sharpened its focus to counter objections based on the separation of powers that the Court had raised in previous cases. By restricting itself to actions relating to the religious rights of prisoners and church-owned lands and by concentrating on its fundamental control over spending and interstate commerce, Congress hoped to avoid the problems that had caused their previous laws to be declared unconstitutional. And indeed, in 2005, the Supreme Court upheld the application of RLUIPA in a case against the State of Ohio.[8]

In Chapter 8, the final chapter, we examine the relationship between these two important institutions that occupy adjacent real estate on Capitol Hill. We discuss how estranged they are and how these stark institutional differences shape their views of the Constitution. One is an institution remarkably open to all sorts of influences; the other is far more isolated. One is inhabited by men and women over who constantly face electoral uncertainty and the possibility of defeat, the other by people with lifetime tenure, who can be removed only by the arduous and seldom-invoked process of impeachment.

One possibly apocryphal anecdote about contrasting views of the Constitution involves either President Grover Cleveland or President Theodore Roosevelt, depending on the storyteller. In it, the president is explaining to a local politician from his party why he is not supporting the politician's bill, explaining that he believes the law the politician seeks is unconstitutional. The politician replies, "What's the Constitution between friends?"[9]

In light of the bitter struggles between Congress and the federal courts, not only over free exercise questions but over a range of emotional, deeply felt, and constitutionally essential issues, the question is now not so much the state of the Constitution between friends but between two important and powerful groups of Americans who may not be enemies but are, ominously, strangers.

Notes

1. David D. Kirkpatrick and Sheryl Gay Stolberg, "How Family's Cause Reached the Halls of Congress," *The New York Times*, March 22, 2005.
2. *Theresa Marie Schindler Schiavo v. Michael Schiavo*, US Court of Appeals for the Eleventh Circuit, No. 05-11628, 10.
3. *Schiavo v. Schiavo*, 4.
4. Laura Parker, "Court Rejects Parents' Potential 'Last Resort'," *USA Today*, March 31, 2005.
5. Carl Hulse and David D. Kirkpatrick, "Even Death Does Not Quiet Harsh Political Fight," *The New York Times,* April 1, 2005.
6. John Cochran, "Legislative Season Drawn in Solid Party Lines," *CQ Weekly*, January 3, 2004, pp. 10–15. On party unity votes (votes that pit a majority of one party against a majority of the other), the average House Democrat voted with the majority of his fellow Democrats 87 percent of the time in 2003. In the Senate, the average Republican voted with other GOP senators 94 percent of the time. In both instances, the level of partisan voting was the highest since the 1960s.
7. *The Federalist on the New Constitution* (Washington DC: Thompson and Homans, 1831), 223.
8. *Cutter et al. v. Wilkinson*, No. 03-9877, May 31, 2005.
9. Louis Fisher, *The Constitution Between Friends* (New York: St. Martin's Press, 1978), v.

STRANGERS ON A HILL

CONGRESS AND THE COURT

1

It All Started with *Marbury*

Visitors to the Georgetown section of Washington DC headed for the Georgetown Mall or the upscale shops and restaurants on the south side of M Street scarcely notice the weathered plaque on the brick building at number 3350, across the street and slightly diagonal from the flashier facade of the Philadelphia Cheesesteak Factory. People familiar with Georgetown's lively night life might remember the building as the home of a night club by the name of Desperadoes. A bronze plaque placed high on the right side of the door of the buff-colored brick house with blue-gray trim proclaims that it houses the Embassy of Ukraine. Below the embassy tablet is another plaque with raised letters that bears the following words:

From 1800 to 1835, residence of William Marbury
Of the legal case Marbury v. Madison. In 1803, through
This case, the United States Supreme Court established
Its right of judicial review of congressional action.

The Madison in the case is James Madison. Arguably the most influential figure in the drafting and defense of the US Constitution, he would later serve as secretary of state and two terms as president. William Marbury, in contrast, comes down to us as a hazy and hapless figure who failed to get a minor judicial post because of a technicality. It is important to remember, however, that this technicality led to what is still one of the Court's most momentous decisions.

Marbury v. Madison has vexed and bedeviled generations of undergraduates suffering through introductory courses in American government or US constitutional law. Even law students with their maturity and greater experience find it a baffling and frustrating case, because so much of the case appears illogical. For example, one of the principal figures in the case, Chief Justice John Marshall, actually changes jobs, and sides, before our very eyes. He appears, moreover, to render a verdict adverse to the interests of the man who nominated him to the high court and to the interests of the Court itself.

The Election of 1800

The contestants in the 1800 election were Charles Pinckney, Thomas Jefferson, Aaron Burr, John Jay, and the incumbent president John Adams, who had succeeded George Washington and was seeking a second term. Adams was a member of Washington's Federalist Party, along with Pinckney, while Jefferson and Burr were both of the Democratic-Republican faction but ran as individuals rather than on a party ticket.

When the electoral votes were counted, one thing was certain: John Adams would no longer be president. He had received sixty-five electoral votes. At first it was less clear who would be president, because both Thomas Jefferson and Aaron Burr came away with seventy-three electoral votes, but after considerable maneuvering, intrigue, and deal-making in the House of Representatives, Jefferson was chosen to be president and Aaron Burr vice president.[1]

One locally influential person who had worked hard for the reelection of John Adams was a thirty-eight-year-old resident of Georgetown named William Marbury.[2] Supporting Adams marked Marbury as an ardent Federalist who could expect little from President Jefferson. Marbury could, however, look forward to a favor from the outgoing president, John Adams. What Marbury had in mind was the post of justice of the peace of the District of Columbia.

Why would Marbury, a self-made man of considerable substance, want to be a justice of the peace?[3] Our image of modern justices of the peace is probably shaped by Hollywood's portrayal of them as bespectacled, elfin figures who perform marriage ceremonies for eloping heiresses. In fact, the office of justice of the peace in 1800 was an important one, because the Justices, sitting *en banc* (as a group), constituted the legislature for Washington DC and performed other important judicial functions.[4]

The Midnight Judges

Until the twentieth amendment to the Constitution took effect on February 6, 1933, a gap of almost five months existed between presidential elections and inauguration day. In one of the final acts of the old one-house Congress created by the Articles of Confederation that preceded the present Constitution, March 4 had been designated as the day that both presidential and congressional terms would begin. What this meant over the next 144 years was that members of Congress and presidents who had been defeated in the fall elections voted and signed bills for four months after having been rejected by the voters. The first beneficiary of this "lame duck" provision was President John Adams.

The loss of the White House was not only a crushing blow to Adams personally but to the Federalist Party that had held power since the Constitution came into force. As historian Page Smith characterized their mood,

> For most Federalists it seemed as if the world, or at least their world had come to an end. Confusion and anarchy must follow the elevation of . . . Jefferson . . . to the presidency.[5]

If Adams could not be president and his Federalist Party could not control the major elective offices of the new republic, they could at least put their mark on appointive positions in the winter of 1800–1801 before their lease ran out on March 4. No appointments were more inviting than judicial posts, especially those with lifetime tenure. By nominating and getting these loyal Federalists confirmed by a Senate still in the hands of his party, Adams could extend his influence beyond the life of his single term in office. Far and away the most important of the posts he sought to fill was the vacancy caused by the resignation of Chief Justice of the Supreme Court Oliver Ellsworth on December 15, 1800.

Eager to fill the post with a reliable Federalist who would serve for life, Adams first offered the job to former Chief Justice John Jay, who had resigned the post in 1795. Jay turned Adams down. After toying with the names of a few elderly jurists, Adams had a mischievous idea. Why not appoint a political enemy of the new president who came from Jefferson's own state of Virginia? The man he chose was Secretary of State John Marshall, who was not only a Virginian but also Jefferson's second cousin. The family tie did not mitigate Marshall's loathing of the new president—a sentiment that Jefferson fully reciprocated.

Marshall was only one of a group of judicial officials whose names Adams sent to the Senate for confirmation. The list read, in Page Smith's words, "like an honor roll of Federalism."[6] The posts, other than that of chief justice of the Supreme Court, had been created by the Federalist-dominated Congress in its waning days at the end of February 1801. Soon after the creation of these offices, Adams called upon John Marshall to assemble a list of nominees for the justice of the peace positions. On that list were, surprisingly, a few members of Jefferson's party, but the greatest number were Federalists—among them, William Marbury.

On March 2, 1801, scarcely two days before leaving office, Adams sent to the Senate the names for confirmation as justices of the peace for the District of Columbia, Marbury among them. The Senate remained in session until nine PM on Tuesday, March 3, in order to confirm the outgoing president's nominees, referred to by Jefferson's partisans as "The Duke of Braintree's Midnight Judges," a sneering reference to the late nominations and Adams's hometown in Massachusetts.[7]

Marbury and the others were duly confirmed. Presidential nominees, upon being approved by a Senate still dominated by Federalists, were entitled to receive formal commissions signed by the president. These are elaborate decorative parchments to which are then affixed the Great Seal of the United States. The custodian of the Great Seal is the Secretary of State, and Marshall worked late into the night of March 3 signing and embossing the commissions with the Great Seal. The Marbury commission was duly sealed and countersigned by Marshall and awaited only delivery to the newly confirmed justice of the peace, whereupon he would assume his place on the bench.

Signed, Sealed, and Undelivered

At this point, it is easy to become confused by the unfolding events, and it helps to step back a bit and recall what has happened. John Marshall is in transition from being Secretary of State to being Chief Justice of the Supreme Court as a result of last-minute action by the outgoing Senate. He is figuratively wearing two hats. It is not surprising, then, that Marshall may have been a trifle overwhelmed, and neglected, as he left his office at the State Department, to order the signed and sealed commissions delivered to a number of the appointees. After all, he was going to be sworn in the next day as chief justice, as was Thomas Jefferson as third president of the United States. One who was not sworn in was William Marbury, whose commission remained, overlooked, at the State Department.

When Jefferson, upon taking office, learned of the undelivered commissions, he directed that they be withheld from the appointees, and he moved to replace the Federalist appointees with people from his own party. James Madison, John Marshall's replacement as Secretary of State, whose name will always be paired with that of William Marbury, did not arrive in Washington until well after Jefferson ordered the commissions to be withheld.[8] When Madison did take office, Marbury demanded the delivery of his commission and Madison refused.

Federalists in Congress took up the cause of Marbury and others who had been denied their commissions. Late in January 1802, a motion was made in the Senate by a Federalist senator that Marbury be furnished with a copy of the record of the proceedings of the Senate for the day that he was confirmed. Jeffersonians opposed the motion, arguing that the journal of executive nominations was kept exclusively for the use of the Senate and could not be given out to anyone except by unanimous consent of the Senate. The Jeffersonian majority had gone so far as to repeal the very law under which Marbury's post and that of most of the other midnight judges had been created. They also turned back a effort to compensate those appointees whose jobs no longer existed.

Mr. Marbury Goes to Court

The denial of the commission was evidently galling to Marbury, who saw his elevation to the post of justice of the peace as the capstone of a career that had made him a wealthy man. He and a number of others who had been denied commissions sought the advice of a prominent lawyer, Charles Lee, a fellow Federalist who had served as attorney general of the United States under both George Washington and John Adams. Lee found a likely remedy for Marbury's problem in Section 13 of the Judiciary Act of 1789, one of the first pieces of legislation passed by the new Congress after the Constitution came into force.

The purpose of the Judiciary Act of 1789 was to establish a court system for the new government under the Constitution. The only court specifically mentioned in the Constitution is the Supreme Court, but the Constitution also says that Congress may "from time to time ordain and establish" courts that are "inferior" to the Supreme Court, and one purpose of the act was to create these lower federal courts.

There is a distinction in the law between courts that have "original jurisdiction" and those that have "appellate jurisdiction" over a case. An example of a court with original jurisdiction over a case is the trial court where the case is first heard—where it was heard originally. Federal District Courts are courts of original jurisdiction. By distinction, courts that hear appeals from the decisions of courts of original jurisdiction are appellate courts, such as the federal Courts of Appeals, also known as "circuit courts." The US Supreme Court is primarily an appellate court, but the

Constitution gives certain limited original jurisdiction to the Supreme Court. The portion of the Judiciary Act that caught Charles Lee's eye when he scanned it for some remedy for William Marbury was an item in Section 13 that gave the Supreme Court a new area of original jurisdiction not enumerated in the Constitution. This was the power to issue a particular kind of legal document known as a writ of *mandamus,* which is an order served on a government official to perform a duty that he is legally obligated to perform but is not performing.[9] Clearly, Madison was obliged to deliver to Marbury the commission for the job for which he had been duly confirmed by the Senate and which had been signed, countersigned, and sealed. It was clear to Charles Lee that the Judiciary Act of 1789 placed a remedy in his hands and that he could force Madison to deliver the commission by going to the Supreme Court and getting them to issue a writ of *mandamus* to compel the recalcitrant secretary of state to perform his obligation under penalty of being in contempt of court.

Justice Marshall Hatches a Scheme

Quite apart from the merit of William Marbury's case, which even many of Jefferson's party members acknowledged, there was a larger political struggle that dwarfed the controversy over the commission and Madison's refusal to deliver it. The Federalists, having lost both the presidency and control of Congress, retained only one outpost in the federal government—the Supreme Court, all of whose members were Federalists. "Scarcely had the wave of popular condemnation passed over them in 1800 when the Federalists determined to make the executive and legislative departments subordinate to the Judiciary."[10]

When Congress changed the dates of the terms in which the Supreme Court could hear cases, the case of William Marbury versus James Madison was delayed by almost two years, until February 1803. Marshall, accordingly, had ample time to ponder the case. Marshall despised Jefferson and all he stood for and would happily have ordered him and Madison to deliver the commission to Marbury, but he also reasoned that they would refuse the order, causing a constitutional crisis. The Federalists, having lost the favor of the voters, would probably lose in a battle over public opinion. Evidently, Marshall never seriously considered issuing the writ of *mandamus*, but he also searched for a way in which his court, the last bastion of Federalism, could establish its supremacy over the elective branches of the government that had fallen into the hands of his political enemies. Was there, indeed, a way in which the Supreme Court could nullify laws that had been passed by Congress and duly signed by the President? The obstacle to Marshall's strategy was the fact that nowhere in the Constitution was any such power granted to the Supreme Court.

What Marshall was toying with was an idea that had surfaced in the debates over the Constitution with the innocuous-sounding name of "judicial review." According to some sources, there was fairly widespread agreement across factional lines in the constitutional debates that courts, by their very nature, would have the power to declare legislative acts unconstitutional if they conflicted with the Constitution. But that power was not explicitly granted to the new Supreme Court in Article III of the Constitution. The closest the Constitution comes is the Supremacy Clause (Article VI), which proclaims that, "This Constitution and the Laws of the United States which shall be made in Pursuance thereof . . . shall be the Supreme Law of the Land."[11]

Marshall did not have to rely solely on the vague wording of Article VI. He found a more lengthy and vigorous defense of judicial review by Alexander Hamilton in *The Federalist* #78, part of that superlative piece of political advocacy that helped to push the Constitution to ratification. Hamilton wrote:

> No legislative act . . . contrary to the constitution can be valid. To deny this, would be to affirm . . . that the representatives of the people are superior to the people themselves.[12]

". . . [I]n sitting down to the preparation of his opinion, [John Marshall] was determined to accomplish a double task—to escape the embarrassment of issuing an order that Jefferson would ignore, and at the same time, in a vital way, to change the then existing concept of American institutions."[13] But what was Marshall proposing to declare unconstitutional in the case that was to come before him, and how would that succeed in establishing the superiority of the Federalist-dominated Supreme Court over a Congress and presidency controlled by the opposition?

For his deft power play, Marshall set his sights on Section 13 of the Judiciary Act of 1789, the provision of the act that gave the Supreme Court the power to issue writs of *mandamus* in cases like Marbury's. Three questions confronted Marshall. The first was whether or not William Marbury was entitled to his commission. If the answer to the first question was "yes," the second was whether the law provided him a way to secure the commission in the face of resistance by Madison. If the answer to the second question was also in the affirmative, and it appeared that the writ of *mandamus* was indeed the remedy, then the only remaining question came down to whether the Supreme Court was the proper authority to issue that writ.

After answering the first two questions in the affirmative and, in course of doing so, administering a rebuke to Jefferson for ordering the commission withheld, Marshall dropped his bombshell. With the unanimous support of the other justices, he declared that, despite the legitimacy of Marbury's claim and the acknowledgment that a writ of *mandamus* was the proper remedy to seek, Section 13 of the Judiciary Act granting the Supreme Court original jurisdiction for the purpose of issuing such writs was in conflict with the Constitution and, hence, "unconstitutional." The Court's reasoning was that "Congress had no authority to redistribute or add to the Court's original jurisdiction,"[14] as set forth in Article III, Section 2 of the Constitution. If Marbury needed relief, he would have to go elsewhere to get it.

There is a paradox here. On the face of it, Marshall is denying to his own Supreme Court the power to issue the writ—a power granted to them by the Judiciary Act of 1789. But in striking down the Supreme Court's power to issue a routine writ on behalf of a relatively minor official, the Court assumed the far greater power to declare part of an act of Congress—a coordinate and coequal branch of the federal government—null and void.

Marbury and Its Aftermath

Immediately after the *Marbury* decision was handed down, there was "scarcely . . . a ripple of public interest. The press was silent. Jefferson had won his point as to the commissions, and the law declared unconstitutional did not interest the people in the least."[15] It might be assumed that once they unsheathed the sword of judicial review of acts of Congress, John Marshall and his fellow Federalists on the Supreme Court wielded it with abandon. In fact, they did not. Jefferson himself anticipated further rulings by the Court against legislation enacted by the Democratic-Republican Congress, but, although the Federalists assailed some actions of the Jeffersonian Congress and administration as unconstitutional, no additional judicial thunderbolts were hurled. Never again in Marshall's tenure did the Court void another act of Congress. Indeed, it was an additional twelve years after Marshall's death before another piece of congressional legislation, the compromise of 1820 setting the northern limit of slavery, was found unconstitutional. Still, to the very end of his life, Jefferson denied the validity of what Marshall had done, believing that the Court's assertion of its prerogative to overturn a decision of the peoples' elected representatives diminished democracy in the United States.

In the 200 years since *Marbury v. Madison*, the Supreme Court has found almost 160 acts of Congress or parts thereof unconstitutional. In recent years, the rulings range in breadth and significance from a 6–3 decision in 2001 finding that the Mushroom Promotion, Research, and Consumer Act violated the First Amendment of the Constitution by "imposing mandatory assessments on mushroom handlers for the purpose of funding generic advertising to promote mushroom sales"[16] to invalidating the Balanced Budget Act, the Flag Protection Act, and the states' ban on first-trimester abortions.

In those latter cases, one might hear the echoes of Thomas Jefferson's complaint that judicial review is fundamentally undemocratic, since it supplants the genius of the people with the putative wisdom of unelected judges. But Congress is not without its tools to retaliate against the Court, and over the last 200 years, Congress has used its own considerable power to pressure the Court into a more compliant posture.

Congressional Leverage on the Supreme Court

From both the personal and institutional perspectives, there are tensions between Congress and the Supreme Court. Those nominated to the Supreme Court must of course present themselves as individuals to the Senate for confirmation. This can be an arduous, even humiliating process.

Our confirmation debates run from the sublime—the famous national seminar on constitutional law conducted during the hearings on Robert Bork's 1987 nomination to the Supreme Court—to the ridiculous—the journalist who thought it would be a great kick, during those same hearings, to publish a list of the films Bork rented at his neighborhood video store.[17]

After the Bork nomination, President Reagan sent to the Senate the name of another federal judge, Douglas Ginsburg, who felt it necessary to telephone the White House to reveal that his wife was once a contestant in a beauty contest and wondered whether this fact would jeopardize his chances for Senate confirmation.[18]

From the perspective of the Senate, the Supreme Court has often appeared as a gang of usurpers in black robes who thwart the will of the people by invalidating the laws enacted by their elected representatives. Typical of Senate reactions to Court decisions was that of Senator James O. Eastland, a Mississippi Democrat, who in the aftermath of the decision in the 1954 case of *Brown v. Board of Education of Topeka* outlawing school segregation warned that the South would not "abide by nor obey this legislative decision by a political court." The "Southern Manifesto" signed by all but three of the senators from the South in reaction to the *Brown* decision deplored the ". . . trend in the federal Judiciary undertaking to legislate, in derogation of the authority of Congress. . . ."[19]

The cyclical relationship between Congress and the Supreme Court over the years since *Marbury* has been marked by periods of sullen mutual tolerance, guarded *laissez-faire*, and outright hostility. If displeasure with decisions by the Court becomes widespread in Congress, there are constitutional means for disciplining a Court that senators and representatives see as too rambunctious. The severest remedy is, of course, impeachment,[20] but there are a number of others.

The requirement that a Supreme Court nominee be approved by a simple majority of the Senate enables Congress to influence the composition of the Court. Since no set number of justices is required by the Constitution, Congress could inflate the number to any size or shrink it drastically.

When Andrew Jackson was on the verge of leaving office, Congress expanded the Court for the first time. During the Civil War, the Court was increased to ten justices, but the number shrank to seven during the administration of Andrew Johnson. The number rose again to nine during the Grant administration and has remained at that number ever since, although in 1937 President Franklin D. Roosevelt and his Democratic allies in the Senate did attempt to pack the Supreme Court by adding a number of new justices, over and above the existing nine, to dilute the voting strength of Court conservatives who opposed his New Deal legislative program.

Another approach favored by those in Congress who wish to curtail the influence of the Court is to have recourse to the provision in Article III, Section 2, of the Constitution that defines the jurisdiction to hear appeals "with such exceptions, and under such regulations as the Congress shall make." Congress can simply eliminate an entire category of appeals that can be heard by the Court. Efforts to limit the Court's appellate jurisdiction have succeeded only once, however, in *Ex Parte McCardle* in 1869, when Congress stripped the Court of its jurisdiction over writs of *habeas corpus.* In 1979 Senator Jesse A. Helms [R-NC] introduced legislation in the Senate that would have denied to federal courts the jurisdiction to hear appeals on cases involving school prayer. The Helms amendment actually passed the Senate 51–40 but was never taken up by the House.[21] The most recent example of "jurisdiction stripping" of the federal courts by Congress was the Graham-Levin Amendment that passed Congress and was signed by President Bush in 2005. It limited the Supreme Court's access to terrorism suspects jailed at the US naval base at Guantánamo Bay, Cuba.

While there is a prohibition in the Constitution against lowering the salaries of federal judges, Congress is under no obligation to raise justices' salaries. In 1964, as a way of punishing the Warren Court for its ruling on apportionment cases, Congress raised the salaries of all top officials in the government except for the members of the Supreme Court. Also considered at the time was a constitutional amendment proposed by Senator Everett M. Dirksen [R-IL] that would have removed all federal court jurisdiction over state legislative redistricting and reapportionment. "Although constitutional amendments require extraordinary majorities that are difficult to mobilize, they are an accepted, legitimate means of reversing the Supreme Court. . . ."[22]

Judicial Review and Free Exercise of Religion

There is one additional remedy at the disposal of Congress when it objects to a Court ruling—to take the decision head-on by passing legislation that seeks to reverse its effect. In 1990, in the case of *Smith v. Employment Division*, when the Supreme Court abandoned a long-held standard for what constituted an abridgment of the free exercise of religion, Congress simply passed a law, the Religious Freedom Restoration Act (REFRA), which restored the old standard that the Court had scrapped. The Court, in turn, retaliated with the very instrument used by John Marshall in *Marbury v. Madison*—judicial review. Thus, the sword of judicial review, first unsheathed by the Supreme Court in that two-century-old case of a disappointed office-seeker, was wielded to challenge Congress's right to define what is meant by the "free exercise of religion." It was not the first such battle between Congress and the courts over this four-word clause, nor the last. And it is this conflict that we will examine in subsequent chapters, to illustrate the larger tensions between these two great institutions of American government. But first, we will take another look back in history to the time before the first real clash between Congress and the courts on this issue and examine the early evolution of the high court's own standard in determining what is meant by "the free exercise of religion."

Notes

1. At the time, the two top vote-getters in a presidential election became president and vice president. There were no candidates designated president and vice president. Maryland ultimately divided its 20 electoral votes, giving five electoral votes each to Jefferson, Adams, Burr, and Pinckney.
2. See: David F. Forte, "Marbury's Travail: Federalist Politics and William Marbury's Appointment as Justice of the Peace," in *Catholic University Law Review,* Winter, 1996.
3. Forte, "Marbury's Travail," 26.
4. Ibid.
5. Page Smith, *John Adams,* Volume 2, 1784–1826 (Garden City, NY: Doubleday, 1962), 1054.
6. Smith, *John Adams,* 1065.
7. Ibid.
8. Forte, "Marbury's Travail," 2.
9. The writ of *mandamus* in the case of *Marbury v. Madison* is certainly the most famous *mandamus* in American history, but these writs are routinely issued for such things as getting judges to recuse themselves from cases in which they have a conflict of interest. Lawyers for the Oklahoma City bomber, Timothy McVeigh, applied for a writ of *mandamus* to compel the federal government to produce documents that had been sealed, claiming that they might aid in McVeigh's defense.
10. Claude G. Bowers, *Jefferson in Power* (Boston: Houghton Mifflin, 1936), 168.
11. Forrest McDonald, *Novus Ordo Seclorum* (Lawrence, KS: University of Kansas Press, 1985), 254–255.
12. Alexander Hamilton, James Madison, and John Jay, *The Federalist on the New Constitution, The Year 1788* (Washington DC: Thompson & Homans, 1831), 334.

13. Bowers, *Jefferson in Power,* 169.
14. Edward Keynes with Randall K. Miller, *The Court vs. Congress* (Durham, NC: Duke University Press, 1989), 97.
15. Ibid
16. *United States v. United Foods, Inc.,* 121 S. Ct. 2334 (2001).
17. Stephen L. Carter, *The Confirmation Mess* (advance uncorrected proofs) (New York: Basic Books, 1994), 6.
18. Ibid., 7
19. Robert Mann, *The Walls of Jericho* (New York: Harcourt Brace, 1996), 155; and Nadine Cohodas, *Strom Thurmond and the Politics of Southern Change* (New York: Simon & Schuster, 1993), 284.
20. Samuel Chase, a member of the Marshall court, remains the only Supreme Court justice ever impeached. Chase's impeachment for alleged crimes dating back to the Adams administration was no doubt also inspired in part by anger in Congress over the Marbury decision. Ultimately, Chase was not removed from office, because the Jeffersonians in the Senate could not muster the constitutionally required two-thirds majority to convict him.
21. David M. O'Brien, *Storm Center: The Supreme Court in American Politics,* 2nd ed. (New York: W. W. Norton, 1990), 362.
22. O'Brien, *Storm Center,* 361, and Keynes, *The Court vs. Congress,* 149.

2

Free Exercise—But How Free?

One piece of legislation introduced in the House of Representatives in 1856 was singularly appropriate in light of the sponsoring Congressman's surname. Rep. Justin S. Morrill saw himself as a moral man indeed. The Morrill Act included strong antipolygamy legislation, and like many Republicans of the time, Morrill regarded a man taking more than one wife as a form of slavery. The specific target of Rep. Morrill's indignation was the Church of Jesus Christ of Latter-Day Saints, better known as the Mormons, who had been practicing polygamy since the 1830s. The Morrill Act was signed into law in 1862 by President Abraham Lincoln.[1]

In October 1874, the leaders of the Mormon Church decided to test the constitutionality of the antipolygamy sections of the Morrill Act by asking George Reynolds, a young Englishman who was serving as private secretary to Brigham Young, the leader of the church, to proclaim his polygamous state and face prosecution. Reynolds was convicted of the initial charges, but his conviction was reversed on appeal because of defects in the grand jury that had indicted him. He was reindicted and convicted, and in 1878 the case came before the Supreme Court of the United States as *Reynolds v. United States*.[2]

The *Reynolds* case involved numerous charges of improper procedures at various stages of his case; only one portion of the Court's opinion written by Chief Justice Morrison R. Waite touches on the controversy that will concern us for the remainder of this book. Waite addressed the question of whether the Morrill Act violated the provision of the First Amendment of the Constitution forbidding Congress from "prohibiting the free exercise" of religion. The power of the Court to review acts of Congress was established, as we have seen, by the decision in *Marbury v. Madison*. Nonetheless, the Reynolds test case was something of a long shot, because in the years between 1803 and 1878, the Court had found unconstitutional only a dozen acts of Congress, none of them touching on controversial religious questions. Indeed, some of the statutory provisions struck down by the Court in those seventy-five years, such as a statute that established a general prohibition on the sale of naphtha, were quite mundane and unmemorable.[3]

The Supreme Court rejected George Reynolds's argument that he took multiple wives because it was his religious duty. Writing for a unanimous court, Chief Justice Waite addressed the question of whether the guarantee in the First Amendment of free exercise of religion excuses conduct that would otherwise be deemed criminal. Waite made a distinction between religious thought and belief on the one hand, and conduct that might result from that set of beliefs. He wrote: "Congress was deprived of all legislative power over mere opinion, but was left free to reach actions which were in violation of social duties or subversive of good order."[4] Waite, perhaps engaging in hyperbole, illustrated that point by saying, "Suppose one believed that human sacrifices were a necessary part of religious worship, would it be seriously contended that the civil government under which he lived could not interfere to prevent a sacrifice?"[5]

The distinction between thought and action as Waite applied it to the free exercise clause of the First Amendment remained settled law for almost a century. Although the Mormons defied federal law and continued to practice polygamy even after successive efforts by Congress to strengthen the Morrill Act, the leadership of the church experienced a change of heart and in

1890 issued a manifesto advising its congregants not to engage in marriages that violated the law of the land. The formal disapproval of the church has not deterred some Mormon men living in isolated communities in the American West from taking more than one wife.

Free Exercise in the States

The very first clause in the Bill of Rights states that "Congress shall make no law respecting an establishment of religion or prohibiting the free exercise thereof." This is a prohibition directed against action by the Congress, and the issue in *Reynolds v. U.S.* was George Reynolds's violation of a law passed by Congress. There has never been any question that Congress cannot establish an official church for the United States nor pass laws prohibiting the free exercise of religion. As the interpreter of the Constitution, the US Supreme Court had the task of determining precisely what these two phrases meant. Whatever the precise meaning of the phrases, however, they were originally meant to apply only to actions by Congress.

In addition, forty-two years after the Bill of Rights was added to the Constitution, Chief Justice John Marshall specifically exempted the states from its constraints. The case, *Barron v. Baltimore*,[6] involved a lawsuit by the owner of a dock in the City of Baltimore, Maryland, whose livelihood had been jeopardized by city improvements that involved the diversion of streams. This diversion caused the water level near his dock to fall, thus making it unsuitable for deep-draft ships to tie up there. He claimed that the City of Baltimore, which was chartered by the State of Maryland, had deprived him of the use of his property without due process of law. The due process clause of the Fifth Amendment clearly forbade the federal government from such an action, but Marshall asserted that if Barron wanted relief he would have to seek it in Maryland's constitution. The Bill of Rights in the US Constitution simply did not apply to actions by the states against individuals.

After the Civil War and the emancipation of the slaves, however, the states of the former Confederacy attempted, in effect, to reimpose slavery by passing "black codes" that severely limited the freedom of black people. In response, Congress passed the Fourteenth Amendment, and the states that had not left the union ratified it. The Fourteenth Amendment prohibits states from infringing on rights guaranteed to citizens by the US Constitution. Those in Congress who had fashioned the amendment certainly believed that its ratification would have the effect of nullifying *Barron v. Baltimore.*

James G. Blaine, a prominent member of Congress at the time, called the Fourteenth Amendment "That provision which establishes American citizenship upon a permanent foundation, which gives to the humblest man in the Republic ample protection against any abridgement of his privileges and immunities by State law. . . ."[7]

Despite the hope of the drafters of the Fourteenth Amendment that it would extend the protection of the Bill of Rights to state actions as comprehensively as it protected individual liberties against encroachments by the federal government, that promise was not soon fulfilled. The combination of a Supreme Court that imposed a narrow and restrictive interpretation on the amendment and the inability of Congress, after the eleven former Confederate states were fully restored to the Union, to pass a civil rights bill, resulted in a piecemeal application of the Fourteenth Amendment to state action. This process, known as "selective incorporation," would require almost 100 years to extend fully the Bill of Rights' mantle of protection. If free exercise of religion was threatened during this period, the most likely aggressors would be the individual states. Indeed, the *Reynolds* case is something of a rarity because of the clear and categorical prohibitions in the Bill of Rights against federal action restricting free exercise. The vast bulk of free exercise cases that we will consider in the remainder of this book originate with actions by state and local governments and bodies such as boards of education and zoning commissions.

The Confrontation on Cassius Street

Residents of New Haven, Connecticut, were probably preoccupied with events in the wider world when they opened their evening papers on May 20, 1940. The Nazi armies were slicing across France and sending the French forces reeling before them. Brussels, the capital of Belgium, had fallen to the invaders, and the beleaguered British and Belgian forces had fallen back to Dunkirk, where a week later 250,000 soldiers would need to be rescued by sea.

At home, President Roosevelt had just requested that Congress appropriate a staggering $2.5 billion to expand the army and navy and proposed that the United States build what seemed the unimaginable figure of 50,000 military aircraft. So if the report of a Supreme Court decision affecting a man named Newton Cantwell and his two sons, Jesse and Russell, was not noticed, it would be understandable.

Residents of the heavily Roman Catholic neighborhood around Cassius Street had come to regard the Cantwells, who proselytized for the Jehovah's Witnesses, as cranks and crackpots. They would appear on the block laden with a sack of books and pamphlets and a portable record player—a wind-up turntable called a phonograph—and a collection of records featuring the recorded voice of the leader of the Jehovah's Witnesses, Joseph Franklin "Judge" Rutherford. As described in an article of the time,

> The usual technique is to map out a city or a rural community and cover it singly or in pairs, porch by porch. Most active members carry a phonograph, which is set, needle poised, before the doorbell is rung. The householder, before he has a chance to turn tail, is met with Judge Rutherford's resonant voice and uncanonical phrases. That, plus the element of surprise, is generally better than a foot in the door."[8]

Quite a few doors were slammed in their faces, but if they did manage to engage the homeowner, they would ask to play a record promoting a book entitled "Enemies." The book contained attacks on the Roman Catholic Church, the religion of most people who lived on the street.

The message of the Cantwells and their determined approach prompted some of the residents of Cassius Street to complain to the local authorities, who found in a Connecticut state law a statute that required people conducting solicitations of the kind pursued by the Cantwells to first obtain the permission of the secretary of the Public Welfare Council, who would determine whether the cause was a legitimate one. If valid, the official would certify the solicitor. Violators of the statute were subject to a $100 fine or thirty days in jail.

On April 26, 1938, Jesse Cantwell approached two men and received their permission to play the record. The record attacked all religions as instruments of Satan but singled out the Catholic religion for particular criticism. While the two men refrained from striking Cantwell, one of them warned him to get off the street before something happened to him. Cantwell was arrested along with his father and brother, and all were found guilty of breach of the peace and of violation of the state law requiring certification of religious solicitations.

The Cantwells appealed their conviction, and the Supreme Court agreed to hear the case. Justice Owen Roberts, writing for the Court's majority, held:

> [T]he statute, as construed and applied to the appellants [the Cantwells], deprives them of their liberty without due process of law in contravention of the Fourteenth Amendment. The fundamental concept of liberty embodied in that Amendment embraces the liberties guaranteed by the First Amendment. The First Amendment declares that Congress shall make no law respecting an establishment of religion or prohibiting the free exercise thereof. The Fourteenth Amendment has rendered the legislatures of the states as incompetent as Congress to enact such laws.[9]

Thus was the free exercise clause of the First Amendment applied to actions by the state, in this case the state legislature of Connecticut, through the Fourteenth Amendment, which the

Court was viewing in a manner much different from the justices of the post–Civil War period.

Justice Roberts, in his opinion, returned to a distinction made by his long-dead predecessor, Justice Waite. Waite had spoken of the distinction between thought and action in the Reynolds case. So did Roberts, sixty-two years later, observing that free exercise "embraces two concepts: freedom to believe and freedom to act. The first is absolute, but in the nature of things, the second cannot be." So while it was impermissible for a state to deny the Cantwell family their right to proselytize, it might well be within a state's legitimate authority to ban other forms of action that sprang from an individual's religious belief. Justice Waite's reflection on the impossibility of approving human sacrifice as a legitimate expression of one's religious belief was, in effect, revisited by Justice Roberts.

One might argue, however, that the Connecticut legislature had a legitimate purpose in halting unscrupulous individuals from attempting to fleece people out of their money—the purpose of the original law requiring official approval of solicitors—and certainly one can imagine all sorts of charlatans exploiting people's faith to make money. Roberts, in his opinion, acknowledged this. Nevertheless, the Court found unacceptable the power given by the law to the secretary of the Public Welfare Council to determine what was, and what was not, a legitimate religious cause. This power to rule on whether or not a solicitation was on behalf of a legitimate religious cause should not, in the Court's view, be vested in a bureaucrat. But the Court left open the possibility that a general regulation that did not target religious groups and applied across the board to all citizens of a state and that touched only tangentially or incidentally on a religious practice might well be allowed.

The cumulative impact of the *Reynolds* and *Cantwell* cases was that all levels of government were constitutionally forbidden to punish citizens for their beliefs but still had full constitutional authority to regulate *actions* of citizens, even those motivated by sincere religious belief, if there was a rational justification for doing so. All things considered, this is not a very exacting limitation on governments. But a series of events twenty years after *Cantwell* and 800 miles distant would raise the bar much higher.

Sabbath in Spartanburg

A substantial portion of court cases dealing with issues of free expression of religion concern religious groups whose practices differ from religions and denominations considered "mainstream." While the definition of mainstream has broadened significantly, there remain rituals, ceremonies, and observances that seem to challenge even the limits of a generally tolerant American public.

Even in a country where a live-and-let-live attitude prevails toward the religious beliefs of individuals, laws enacted by governments at all levels generally don't take into account the practices of adherents of non-Christian denominations or Christian denominations with unconventional doctrines and practices. Government officials, such as those in Connecticut in the Cantwell case, are charged with enforcing the letter of the law, and this often leaves little room for those whose manner of worship does not fit neatly into codes or regulations easily observed by the majority. So it was with a young woman whose job was to tend spools at the Beaumont Division of Spartan Textile Mills in Spartanburg, South Carolina.

The young woman, then known by her maiden name, Adell Hoppes, first started working at Spartan Mills in 1924 as a twenty-two-year-old, but by then she was already an experienced millhand, having begun work at the age of eleven in Cowpens, South Carolina. Textile factories at the time were hard places to work. They were the "dark satanic mills" of which William Blake wrote in his hymn "Jerusalem." A photograph taken by the renowned photographer Lewis Hine shows a young woman employed as a millhand in Spartanburg; the viewer is touched by her youth and innocence. The picture was shot a few years before

Adell Hoppes began work—otherwise it might have been an image of Adell herself.

She worked in the Beaumont Mill from 1924 until 1959. She had married and was now Adell Sherbert. In 1959, she was dismissed for refusing to work a Saturday shift. The mill had recently increased production and raised the workweek from five days to six. She declined to work because she was a member of the Seventh-day Adventist Church, whose doctrines designate Saturday as the Sabbath, because it was on that day that Jesus, a Jew, would have observed the day of rest.

The Adventists are an offshoot of the Baptists, established as a separate denomination in the 1840s. They were initially known as "Millerites" after their founder William Miller, who preached the imminent return of Jesus to earth and set the date of his second coming at October 22, 1844, based upon an interpretation of the words of the prophet Daniel. When the date arrived and Jesus did not appear, much of the group left the movement. The remainder, led by Ellen G. White, reestablished the Group as the Seventh-day Adventist Church.

On July 5, 1959, when the six-day workweek was instituted at Spartan Mills. Sherbert continued as before to work her five-day week but absented herself for the first six Saturdays. The mill gave her three warnings that her refusal to work would lead to her dismissal. At that time she was a widow with five children taking home a weekly paycheck of $32.56. She attempted to find work in three other mills but found that all were on a six-day-a-week schedule.

On July 28, 1959, Adell Sherbert was fired. She immediately applied for unemployment compensation, but on September 4 her claim was denied by a claims examiner of the South Carolina Employment Security Commission. She appealed the decision to an appeals board, which upheld the examiner's decision to deny Sherbert the benefits. On January 5, 1960, Sherbert took her case to the Court of Common Pleas of Spartanburg County for a judicial review of the Commission's decision, but here too she lost. Judge J. Woodrow Lewis issued his decision on June 27, 1960, holding that because of her refusal to work on Saturday, she had made herself unavailable for work, and under the South Carolina Unemployment Compensation Law this meant she could not claim benefits. Sherbert appealed once again, this time to the state's highest court, the Supreme Court of South Carolina. The defendants were the members of the South Carolina Employment Security Commission, headed by its chairman, Charlie V. Verner. Her appeal in the case of *Sherbert v. Verner* was rejected on May 17, 1962. Chief Justice Moss, writing for the South Carolina Supreme Court in its 3–1 decision, recalled:

> This statute [the unemployment compensation law] was passed in 1936, at a time when this state . . . was suffering from a prolonged depression which had resulted in industry laying off many workers. . . . This unquestionably was the evil which the legislature was seeking to remedy . . . I find nothing in the act itself or in the circumstances surrounding its passage to indicate an intention to . . . provide benefits for a worker compelled to give up his job because of a change in his personal circumstances.[10]

Moss went on to say that the beneficial purposes of unemployment compensation would be undercut "if benefits were paid to persons who became unemployed, not because the employer could no longer provide them with work but solely because of changes in their personal circumstances." He then dismissed with little comment Sherbert's claim that the state's unemployment compensation law violated her free exercise of religion.[11]

Adell Sherbert then took the next step and appealed her case to the US Supreme Court. It took less than a year for the court to agree to take the case. It was argued before the court on April 24, 1963, by attorney William D. Donnelly. A number of Jewish groups filed *amicus curiae* briefs in support of Sherbert's appeal; such "friend of the court" briefs are filed by those who are not directly involved in the case but have an interest in the outcome. It is not surprising that Jewish groups filed such briefs, because they share observance of the Sabbath with the Adventists. South Carolina was defended by that state's attorney general, Daniel R. McLeod.

According to Sherbert's son Frank, interviewed in 2002, this unemployed widow with five children was able to conduct a lengthy court battle because of help from her church. "I think it was mostly the [Seventh-day Adventist] Church that asked her to go through with this. They wanted to take it to [the Supreme] Court."[12]

The expenses of these so-called test cases are often underwritten by groups who have an interest in the outcome. In this instance, the Seventh-day Adventist Church was hoping that Adell Sherbert's appeal would succeed, because if she prevailed, the members of the denomination would be shielded from dismissal for declining to work on Saturday.

A Compelling State Interest

On June 17, 1963, almost four years to the day after Spartan Mills imposed its six-day work week, the US Supreme Court by a 5–4 vote held that the denial of unemployment benefits to Sherbert restricted her free exercise of religion. Justice William Brennan, writing for the majority, asked "whether some compelling state interest" in the eligibility provisions of the unemployment law justified restricting Sherbert's right of free exercise of her religion under the First Amendment. He answered by quoting from another case that "only the gravest abuses, endangering paramount interests, give occasion for permissible limitation."

He then briefly addressed a point that had not even been made by the South Carolina Supreme Court but had been added by Attorney General McLeod in his arguments, that numerous false claims for unemployment compensation would draw down the jobless fund. Brennan derided the claim, saying ". . . Even if the possibility of spurious claims did threaten to dilute the fund . . . it would plainly be incumbent on [the state of South Carolina] to demonstrate that no alternative forms of regulation would combat such abuses without infringing First Amendment rights."[13]

In addition to reaffirming the principle laid down in the *Cantwell* case, referred to in the Court's holding in *Sherbert v. Verner*, that neither the federal government nor the states could punish individuals for their beliefs, the decision in the *Sherbert* case undercut the distinction between belief and action laid down by Justice Waite in the *Reynolds* case. But, above all, it was the high bar that the Court erected against any action by a state to curtail the free exercise of religion that made Adell Sherbert's victory so significant. To assert that a state needed to have a compelling interest to restrict religious practice, as opposed to a rational justification, was to reduce drastically the ability of a state to control the behavior of a believer acting on genuine religious conviction. Such actions would obviously not include practices like human sacrifice or the refusal to pay taxes.

There was a significant dissent in the case by Justice John M. Harlan, who observed that the intent of the South Carolina unemployment compensation law was not to interfere with the religious practices of the state's citizens. The law applied to everyone in South Carolina who was unemployed.

> The fact that . . . personal considerations sprang from [Sherbert's] religious convictions was wholly without relevance to the state court application of the [unemployment compensation] law. Thus, in no proper sense can it be said that the State discriminated against [Sherbert] on the basis of her religious beliefs or that she was denied benefits *because* she was a Seventh-day Adventist. She was denied benefits just as any other claimant would be denied benefits who was not "available for work" for personal reasons.[14]

Harlan's argument, simply stated, is that on the face of it, the South Carolina unemployment compensation law was neutral on the subject of an applicant's religion, that it was certainly not targeting people who were observant, and that the statute applied generally to every unemployed South Carolinian. Although Harlan did not say so in so many words, he suggested that the law could not be blamed for Adell Sherbert's having been caught up in it. Another decade would pass before the Court had the opportunity to speak out again on a free exercise question and provide added substance to the compelling state interest test in the case of *Wisconsin v. Yoder*.[15]

As for Adell Sherbert, the victory was not an unqualified triumph. Interviewed on the day of the Supreme Court decision, she said, "It makes me feel good," but she quickly added that it couldn't help her find a job. "This is the only work I know. I've tried and tried to find work, but it seems every place works on Saturday."[16]

Having long ago exhausted the unemployment benefits she had won, Adell Sherbert eked out an existence by babysitting and continued to live in the small house on Southern Street just behind the mill that had been sold to her by Beaumont Mills in 1956. In a strange turn of fate, the children she most often cared for were the grandchildren of the owner of the mill from which she was fired. On the occasion of her death, on December 12, 1989, the Spartanburg *Herald-Journal* ran a five-paragraph obituary. It made no mention of the central role she had played in one of the most important cases in American constitutional law.

Readin', Ritin', and Religion

Less than decade after the Supreme Court's ruling in *Sherbert v. Verner*, it had occasion to render another verdict in a case that once again dealt with the unconventional practices of a religious group outside the theological mainstream.

From the perspective of doctrine, the Amish (sometimes referred to as "Pennsylvania Dutch") have little in common with the Mormons, Jehovah's Witnesses, and Seventh-day Adventists other than the fact they are all Christians. Part of a larger group known as Anabaptists, which includes various groups of Mennonites, the Amish shun many of the trappings of modernity, including motor vehicles and electricity. Scornful of personal ornamentation, they refer to themselves as "The Plain People." They are resolute pacifists and refuse military service. So deep-seated is their pacifism that, although all married men grow beards, they refuse to wear mustaches because they are "the badges of a soldier." Among other things, they refuse to salute the flag (they consider any flag an ungodly symbol) or educate their children beyond elementary school. The beliefs of the Amish, not surprisingly, have led to occasional clashes with the larger world beyond their communities.

The clash for Jonas Yoder, Wallace Miller, and Adin Yutzy of Green County, Wisconsin, came in 1970 with their decision not to send their children to school after they had completed the eighth grade, in violation of Wisconsin's compulsory school attendance laws that required schooling until the age of sixteen. The Yoder, Miller, and Yutzy children were ages fourteen and fifteen. The refusal of the three families to send the children to school beyond eighth grade was based upon the Epistle of St. Paul to the Romans that they "not be conformed to the world." And while the Amish did not object to schooling up to the eighth grade because of the basic skills learned by the child during that stage of education, they rejected any higher level of schooling as "promoting values they rejected as influences that alienate man from God."[17]

The Amish families were charged, tried, and convicted of violating the state's compulsory attendance law and were each fined $5.00. The court found that the school attendance law did, in fact, interfere with the Amish families' freedom to act in accordance with their religious beliefs, but concluded that the requirement that children be schooled until sixteen was a "reasonable and constitutional" exercise of government power. The families appealed to the Wisconsin Circuit Court, which affirmed the convictions, but on appeal to the state's highest court, the Wisconsin Supreme Court, the conviction and fine were thrown out. The State of Wisconsin then asked the US Supreme Court to review the case, which was argued before the Court on December 8, 1971.

A Balancing Act

In a 7–0 decision (two justices, Lewis Powell and William Rehnquist, took no part in the consideration of the case), the US Supreme Court upheld the decision of the Wisconsin Supreme Court that the state had failed to sustain its case that its interest in "establishing and maintaining an educational system" trumped the Amish families' right to the free exercise of their religion. In other words, in balancing the interests of the State of Wisconsin in ensuring the proper education of its children and the Amish families' refusal to sanction education beyond the eighth grade, the First Amendment right of free exercise of religion weighed more heavily. The justices did not say that no state interest could ever be compelling, nor on the other hand did they say that in all instances the free exercise of religion would triumph over any conceivable interest of the state. In this particular instance, however, they found that, on balance, the state's interest was insufficiently compelling as compared to the religious imperatives of the Amish.

The combined force of the *Sherbert* and *Yoder* decisions was to compel all levels of government, before infringing on the activities of any religious group, to meet the stringent and exacting standard that they had a compelling reason to do so.

Unlike the *Reynolds* case, neither the *Sherbert* nor the *Yoder* decisions involved federal law. Both grew out of the extension by the Fourteenth Amendment of Bill of Rights protections against state actions that was established in the *Cantwell* case, through the process of selective incorporation by the Supreme Court. In no case was a law found to be unconstitutional, although the applications of both the South Carolina unemployment statute and the Wisconsin compulsory attendance law were found to be improper in light of their interference with principled religious behavior. It appeared, moreover, that an unshakable standard had been set for states to meet, but in less than a decade, a sizeable crack would develop in that foundation, and in less than another ten years, it would suffer total demolition at the hands of the US Supreme Court. That decision would cause Congress to be arrayed against the Supreme Court, and a great pageant of constitutional checks and balances would unfold.

Notes

1. Edwin Brown Firmage and Richard Colin Mangrum, *Zion and the Courts: A Legal History of the Church of Jesus Christ of Latter-day Saints, 1830–1900* (Urbana, IL: University of Illinois Press, 1988), 130–31.

2. US 98:145 [1878].
3. *US v. DeWitt* [1870].
4. *Reynolds v. US,* 98 US 145 [1879]
5. Ibid.
6. 7 Pet. (32 US) 243 [1833].
7. James G. Blaine, *Twenty Years of Congress,* Vol. 2 (Norwich, CT: The Henry Bill Publishing Co., 1886), 312.
8. Stanley High, "Armageddon, Inc.," *Saturday Evening Post,* September 14, 1940, 58.
9. *Cantwell v. The State of Connecticut* 310 US 296 (1940).
10. *Sherbert v. Verner* 240 S.C. 286 (1962).
11. Ibid.
12. Interview with Frank Sherbert, July 2, 2002, Spartanburg, SC, by Betsy Wakefield Teter, Executive Director, Hub City Writers' Project.
13. *Sherbert v. Verner,* 37 US 398.
14. Ibid.
15. 406 US 205 (1972).
16. "Highest Court OK's Spartan's Jobless Pay," *Spartanburg Herald-Journal* June 18, 1963.
17. Leo Pfeffer, *Religion, State, and the Burger Court* (Buffalo, NY: Prometheus Books, 1984), 59. Pfeffer filed an *amicus curiae* brief in the *Yoder* case on behalf of the Synagogue Council of America.

3

Sherbert, Melting

Thus far in our account, Congress and the Supreme Court are
at peace over the meaning of free exercise of religion. The
legal conflicts involve actions by the states that the Supreme
Court has interpreted as infringing on the rights of individuals
in the conduct of their religion—Connecticut against the Cantwells proselytizing, South Carolina against Adell Sherbert's
avoidance of Saturday work in the mill, and Wisconsin against the
determination of the Amish to limit schooling to eight years.

Moreover, in the two decades after it was decided, the test of
"compelling state interest" as laid down in the *Sherbert* case had
attained the comfortable status of what attorneys refer to as "settled law." It laid out with unmistakable clarity the conditions governments had to meet before they could limit the free exercise of
religion.

From the year of the *Sherbert* decision, 1963, until the mid-
1980s, "The . . . Court consistently applied the *Sherbert* compelling interest test. . . . Moreover, in each free exercise decision,
the Court cited *Sherbert* and *Yoder* as controlling precedent."[1] It
appeared, then, as if the compelling state interest test as applied to
official infringements on the free exercise of religion had been
carved in stone, and that governments would, in the future, have
to examine scrupulously any law or regulation for any provision,
however inconsequential or incidental, that interfered with the
free exercise of religion.

While court decisions or principles of law may sometimes seem immutable, courts are not. The Supreme Court is certainly no exception. During the twenty-year period after the *Sherbert* decision, seven of the nine justices who heard the case died. The only survivors by the mid-1980s were William J. Brennan, who wrote the *Sherbert* opinion, and Byron White, one of the two dissenters in the case. The most significant retirement was that of Chief Justice Earl Warren, who had been part of the *Sherbert* majority. He was replaced as Chief Justice by Warren E. Burger in 1969. The fact that seven new pairs of eyes are scrutinizing a case opens the possibility that they will see it very differently from a previous Supreme Court.

The *Sherbert* decision stood, almost unmodified, for more than twenty years. When it fell, however, it fell resoundingly. When overturned, it created in American politics a jolt equivalent to a major earthquake. But, as in the modern science of geophysics, it was possible to detect early rumblings that gave warnings that a vastly changed court and a case with circumstances and litigants different from *Sherbert* might trigger an upheaval. The early rumblings that roiled the placid terrain created by *Sherbert* were from a case that reached the Supreme Court on appeal from the US District Court of Western Pennsylvania. It was the case of *US v. Lee*.

The Compelling Nature of Taxes

As in the *Yoder* case, the 1982 case of *United States v. Lee*[2] involved members of the Amish community. This case had its beginnings in the very heartland of the Amish, the state of Pennsylvania. Edwin Lee, the defendant in the case, like so many Amish men, was a carpenter who built furniture. He also owned a furniture shop and employed other Amish carpenters.

Employers in establishments of all sizes, even households that employ a single house cleaner, are required to contribute to Social Security for salaried employees—the item on a pay stub labeled "FICA." Lee declined to withhold from his employees' paychecks the Social Security tax or to make the employer's contribution.

He maintained that the payment of the Social Security tax violated his and his employees' religious beliefs, which held that it was the responsibility of members of the community, not the government, to contribute to the welfare of their neighbors. What Lee was arguing was that the free exercise of religion of his Amish workers was being interfered with by the federal government and the Social Security System created by act of Congress in 1935.

When, in 1978, Lee was assessed more than $27,000 by the Internal Revenue Service for seven years of unpaid Social Security taxes, he sent the IRS $91 and then sued for a refund in US District Court, claiming that the Social Security taxes violated his right to free exercise of religion under the First Amendment.

The District Court in Pennsylvania held that the Social Security taxes were unconstitutional when applied to the Amish and cited a federal statute that the judge interpreted as applying to religious groups. The US Government appealed the District Court decision directly to the Supreme Court. The case was argued on November 2, 1981, and on February 23, 1982, a unanimous Supreme Court reversed the decision of the District Court.

The justices held that the exemption cited by the District Court applied only to individuals and not to businesses. More generally, however, they concluded that the payment of Social Security taxes was, in fact, a compelling state interest because the Social Security system is "nationwide . . . [and] mandatory participation is indispensable to the fiscal vitality of the . . . system." Then, quoting from a Senate report, the justices stated flatly that "Widespread individual voluntary coverage under social security . . . would undermine the soundness of the social security program."[3]

The Court also took pains to distinguish *US v. Lee* from *Wisconsin v. Yoder* by saying that while it was possible to make exceptions in the case of schooling, the duty to pay Social Security tax is no different from paying income tax, and even though the objection to paying the Social Security levy was based on a principled objection, "the broad public interest in maintaining a sound tax system is of such a high order [that] religious belief in conflict with the payment of taxes affords no basis for resisting the tax."[4]

The test to be applied by courts as set forth in *Sherbert v. Verner* was that the "required degree of accommodation [of religious practices by governments] is to be determined by balancing the religious interest against the regulatory interest."[5] In the matter of Yoder and his objections to schooling beyond a certain grade, the judges held up the scales and saw them tip in Yoder's favor. In the matter of Lee, the same balancing act resulted in a decision against free exercise. The thumb on the scale was the compelling state interest that the justices saw in *Lee* that they did not see in *Yoder.*

A comment that might well have passed unnoticed in a concurring opinion by Justice John Paul Stevens in the *Lee* case turned out to be most prophetic as far as the future of the *Sherbert* standard and all free exercise cases were concerned. While agreeing with the basic decision to reverse the lower court decision and remand the case to the District Court where the trial was first conducted, Stevens added this sentence: "In my opinion, it is the objector who must shoulder the burden of demonstrating that there is a unique reason for allowing him a special exemption from a valid law of general applicability."[6]

What is a "valid law of general applicability"? It is simply a law that applies to everyone. In the context of the free exercise of religion clause of the First Amendment, it is a law not aimed at restricting free exercise. The enforcement of such a law, however, might have some incidental and unintended impact on religion. A law forbidding murder, for example, would curtail the free religious expression of a cult that practiced human sacrifice. Where Stevens departed from the rest of the Court majority in *Lee* was in denying that the government even needed to make a case for a compelling state interest in Amish workers' paying payroll taxes. "What was needed, in his judgment, was a different constitutional standard."[7] Nonetheless, the old standard remained intact, and any governmental authority that infringed on free exercise would still need to meet the compelling state interest test.

A few years after the payment of Social Security taxes was deemed to be a compelling state interest, another judicial balancing act was performed in an unusual situation, and once again the Court found another government interest compelling. Congress, pointedly, did not. This time the government authority was the US Air Force and the issue touched on a core value of the military, a concept known as "good order and discipline."

Hats Off to the Air Force

Simcha Goldman was an Orthodox Jew and an ordained rabbi who enrolled in a program offered by the US Air Force. Under the terms of the Armed Forces Health Professions Scholarship Program, he could go to school and have his tuition and books paid for and a monthly stipend for the time required to achieve his degree, a doctorate in psychology. While in school, students in this program were placed on inactive reserve status in the air force. Upon receiving the degree, they were obliged to spend one year on active duty for each year their education was subsidized. Goldman took up his religious duties at the mental health clinic at March Air Force Base near Riverside, California, where he was a clinical psychologist.[8]

For a time while he was at March AFB, Goldman wore, in addition to the regulation officer's uniform and service cap, a yarmulke under the military hat. The yarmulke is a skullcap worn by observant Jewish men obeying the biblical injunction to cover their heads. While seeing patients in the clinic, Goldman would remove his military headgear and wear only the skullcap. Outside on the base, his yarmulke was concealed under the military cap.[9]

This arrangement went unchallenged for some time, but in 1981, Goldman was called to testify for the defense in a court-martial. He appeared at the court-martial wearing the yarmulke but not the regulation headgear over it. He was challenged by the prosecutor, who filed a complaint with the commanding officer arguing that Goldman's wearing of the religious cap violated air force uniform regulations that prohibit the wearing of headgear indoors except for military police on duty.

Goldman was ordered by the commanding officer not to wear the yarmulke outside the clinic where he worked. Goldman refused and had his attorney protest the order to the General Counsel of the air force. The commanding officer then forbade Goldman to wear the yarmulke even inside the clinic. Goldman's offer to show up for work in civilian clothing was rebuffed by the commanding officer, who followed up the rejection with a formal letter of reprimand and a warning that continued defiance of the order might lead to a court-martial for Goldman.

For the air force, the problem was not the fact that the headgear in question was an article of Jewish religious apparel, but that it was being worn indoors. Military regulations require personnel to remove caps when entering a building. The prohibition, then, would have applied to a turban or a kaffiyeh. The sole exception for on-duty air force personnel is members of the military police. For Goldman, the issue was the free exercise of his religion, which requires the wearing of head covering at all times, and he responded by filing suit, naming Secretary of Defense Caspar Weinberger as defendant.

Thus began the case of *Goldman v. Weinberger*. The repercussions of this case would go far beyond either *Yoder* or *Lee*, and its political impact would exceed even *Sherbert*, because the *Goldman* case, for the first time in the twentieth century, put the Supreme Court and Congress on a collision course and led to a dramatic struggle over which branch of government had the power to define constitutional rights and liberties.

What Goldman was seeking was an *injunction* against the Secretary of Defense, a legal remedy that asks, not for damages, but for a court order that either forbids an official from discharging some duty or commands that person to perform a duty. A US District Court granted Goldman's request for an injunction, because in the opinion of the judge his claim that his free exercise of religion was being curtailed was likely to triumph over the claim of the air force. The judge noted that the dispute involved a departmental regulation, not a statute passed "by a coequal branch of government." In short, the court was not butting heads with

Congress. The judge appeared to make light of the Pentagon's position that allowing Goldman to wear his yarmulke "will crush the spirit of uniformity, which in turn will weaken the will and fighting ability of the US Air Force."[10]

Almost simultaneously, another case involving the wearing of a yarmulke reached another US District Court.[11] The judge in the second case chose to side with the air force, thus creating a conflict that would have to be reconciled by a higher court. In this case, it was the US Court of Appeals for the District of Columbia, which is regarded as the most prestigious federal court below the Supreme Court and from which a number of Supreme Court nominees have been chosen.

A panel of three judges from the Court of Appeals resolved the dispute in favor of the court that had sided with the air force. The judges accepted the assertion by the air force that if it allowed an exception to the rule forbidding headgear other than official caps, it would also be obliged to allow a range of religious garb ranging from the turbans and daggers of Sikhs to the dreadlocks of Rastafarians.

Goldman's attorney petitioned to have the case reheard by the Appeals Court *en banc*, meaning the case would be presented again, not to the three-judge panel, but to the entire DC Appeals Court, consisting of eleven judges. The appeal for a rehearing was denied, and a vigorous dissent from the denial was issued by one of the judges on the US Court of Appeals for the District of Columbia, Judge Antonin Scalia, who would be named to the US Supreme Court in 1986 by President Reagan. In his dissent, Scalia invoked the standard set forth in *Sherbert v. Verner* that what the air force had done had burdened Goldman's free exercise of religion without a compelling state interest.

The decision by the DC Circuit Court brought an immediate reaction from religious groups. Because of the prestige of the DC Circuit Court, the decision not to rehear Goldman's appeal was especially alarming to these groups, even though the ultimate constitutional authority, the Supreme Court, had not yet considered the case. Groups alarmed by the decision turned to the one part of the federal government uniquely responsive to popular demands, the US Congress.

Unlike the courts, which cannot be lobbied directly, Congress is the place where, in the words of the First Amendment, people come to "petition the government for a redress of grievances." The Goldman case generated considerable grievance. The impulse for remedial action came, not surprisingly, from Orthodox Jews. Also, not surprisingly, their champion in Congress was a member whose constituency comprised the largest community of observant Jews in the United States.

Steven J. Solarz was, in 1984, a forty-four-year-old Democrat in his fifth term in the House. His constituency, New York's thirteenth, was, geographically, one of the nation's smallest congressional districts.

> Seldom more than a mile wide, it extends far enough that it would take you most of working day to drive through it. . . . It has Hasidic neighborhoods in the north, burgeoning Orthodox communities in Borough Park and along Ocean Parkway, and neighborhoods brimming with new Jewish emigrants from Soviet Russia in Brighton Beach and Coney Island on the Ocean. The thirteenth is basically the poor Jewish district, one of the few majority Jewish districts in the nation and the home of many of the nation's least affluent Jewish communities.[12]

Solarz was first made aware of the *Goldman* case and inspired to take legislative action by Nathan Lewin, Goldman's attorney. Lewin had a long-standing interest in religious questions. As Solarz recollected the sequence of events:

> Nat Lewin was the one who suggested the legislation, and I was only too happy to introduce it, first, because I agreed in principle that he should be allowed to wear a yarmulke on duty, but also because I represented a very large constituency of orthodox and Hasidic Jews. So it was a principle that was warmly endorsed by my constituents.[13]

In 1984 Solarz introduced an amendment to the defense authorization bill that would have required the military services to allow their personnel to wear religious headgear when their faith required it. During a one-year trial period, the military could reinstate the ban if it was found that military performance was impaired. The authorization bill passed the House with the Solarz amendment, but the amendment was deleted by the House-Senate conference committee.[14] A conference committee is a joint committee set up to deal with differences between the House and Senate versions of a bill. Because the presentment clause of the Constitution requires Congress to submit a single bill to the president for his approval or his veto, any differences between the House and Senate versions need to be reconciled by a conference committee.

All that survived of Solarz's first effort was a provision requiring the Defense Department to report to Congress on what changes the military might make in its regulations that would better promote free expression of religion within the ranks. The change in the law was a minor incremental adjustment that did not really provide any relief for Goldman. Accordingly, Goldman took the next step.

He appealed to the US Supreme Court, and on March 25, 1986, the court handed down a decision by a vote of 5–4. It upheld the ruling of the DC Circuit and supported the position of the air force.[15]

Not surprisingly, Goldman's attorney, Nathan Lewin, in his oral argument before the Court, invoked the compelling interest standard laid down in *Sherbert v. Verner* and *Yoder*. Justice Rehnquist, who wrote for the majority, rejected Lewin's arguments that the compelling state interest test ought to be applied to Goldman's situation. Rehnquist argued that the military is simply different, that Adell Sherbert and Jonas Yoder were civilians, and as Rehnquist stated:

> Our review of military regulations challenged on First Amendment grounds is far more deferential than constitutional review of similar laws or regulations designed for civilian society.

The desirability of dress regulations in the military is decided by the appropriate military officials, and they are under no constitutional mandate to abandon their considered professional judgment.[16]

A spirited dissent was made by Justice William Brennan, who made the initial argument that in rejecting Goldman's claim, the Supreme Court majority had evaded its responsibility to protect basic constitutional rights and had been gullible in its acceptance of the arguments of the military about the importance of good order and discipline. As a parting shot, Brennan called upon Congress to "correct this wrong."

Congress Steps In

Article I, Section 8 of the Constitution empowers Congress "To make rules for the government and regulation of the land and naval forces." Accordingly, Rep. Solarz was on solid constitutional ground in 1986 when he introduced a new amendment, as he had been when he introduced the first one in 1984. Opponents did make some familiar objections. One colleague raised the possibility that religious groups with even more distinctive and obtrusive headgear would surely demand the same right to wear it in the military. Solarz thought this objection raised some intriguing possibilities.

> I remember that someone asked me when I introduced it, What about Sikhs? My response was that it was well known that the Sikhs had a strong military tradition, and the best thing we could do to redress the imbalance of forces between NATO and the Warsaw Pact in Europe would be to recruit two Sikh divisions and put them in the Fulda Gap in Germany.[17]

This time, the amendment passed the House but ran up against strong opposition in the Senate from the military, veterans, and patriotic organizations. Defense Secretary Caspar Weinberger also released a letter signed by the uniformed chiefs of all the military services and the Chairman of the Joint Chiefs of Staff, all five of whom were four-star generals. It came to be known as the "Twenty-Star Letter," but it failed to kill the amendment. Some senators switched the votes they had first cast against the Solarz amendment. Even more significant, however, in the legislation's success were the votes of eight new Democratic senators, elected in 1986. The result was that in 1987 the military was authorized by Congress to allow the wearing of items of religious garb while in uniform, providing that the Secretary of Defense does not determine that the garment interferes with the performance of the soldier.[18]

After the bill was signed by President Reagan, Nathan Lewin, who had pleaded the case both in the Circuit Court and before the Supreme Court and had assisted Rep. Solarz in the drafting of the amendment to the Defense Authorization Bill, had lunch with Supreme Court Justice William Brennan, who had written the dissent in the *Goldman* case and invited Congress to neutralize the effect of the Court's ruling. Brennan had been invited to Israel to receive an honorary degree from the Hebrew University and wanted Lewin's suggestions about people he might speak to while in the country.

As Lewin recalled the conversation, Brennan said that he had received a letter from Rep. Solarz informing him of the passage of the bill and enclosing a yarmulke made of camouflage material that had been worn by a Jewish army chaplain during the Grenada invasion in 1983. Brennan told Lewin:

> You know, Nat, I read Solarz's letter and I put the yarmulke on my head, and then I forgot I was wearing it, and I wore it the rest of the day in my chambers in the Supreme Court. My law clerks were sort of astounded. I walked through their offices and my secretary's office and they couldn't understand why. And it wasn't until a couple of minutes after I got home that my wife said to me, "Hey, what have you got on your head?" It was only then that I realized that I had been wearing the yarmulke all day.[19]

The response to the *Goldman* cases by the House and Senate demonstrated that Congress was willing to challenge the Supreme Court as the sole expositor of First Amendment rights, but it did so in an area that was uniquely within its own constitutional province. The power of Congress to make regulations governing the armed forces was difficult for the Court to challenge, but the acquiescence of the Court to the Congress in a case involving the military provided no clue as to how the Court would respond to infringement of an individual's free exercise of religion when that person was a civilian. The *Goldman* case, because it involved the military, did not really seem to undermine the compelling state interest standard, and even the sharpness of the questions directed at Goldman's attorney by Justice Rehnquist did not suggest to him that the *Sherbert* standard was in jeopardy, nor that the justices had been antagonized by efforts to get Congress to enact legislation nullifying the two *Goldman* decisions.[20]

It would not take long, however, for the Supreme Court to speak out boldly on the subject and engaged with Congress in a series of monumental battles over which institution would have the definitive word on the meaning of the free exercise clause of the Constitution. It would come in a case that was not affected by the complicating factor of the distinctive needs of the US military. It would involve a very different set of litigants and a set of religious practices that were of a decidedly exotic and controversial nature.

What was the state of the law on free exercise at the end of the 1980s? Compelling state interest remained the justification that governments—both state and federal—would have to prove if their actions infringed on religious exercise. A notable example of what constituted compelling state interest had been provided in the form of the withholding tax for Social Security by the *Lee* case. Religious scruples could not trump the federal government's requirement for a universal system of old-age and survivors' insurance. Moreover, even the most vigilant defender of religious liberty could not plausibly make the case that Social Security withholding targeted religions. Congress had acted within its proper sphere to challenge the Supreme Court in the Goldman case. The battle over free exercise, its reach, and its limitations, had yet to be fully joined.

Notes

1. Carolyn N. Long, *Religious Freedom and Indian Rights* (Lawrence, KS: University of Kansas Press, 2000), 60.
2. 455 US 252 (1982).
3. Ibid.: the ellipses in the quotation from the Senate report are from the Supreme Court decision.
4. Ibid.
5. Mark Tushnet, *Red, White, and Blue* (Cambridge, MA: Harvard University Press, 1988), 264–65.
6. *US v. Lee.*
7. Tinsley E. Yarborough, *The Rehnquist Court and the Constitution* (New York: Oxford University Press, 2000), 174.
8. *Goldman v. Weinberger, Secretary of Defense, et al.* 475 US 503 (1986).
9. Ibid.
10. Louis Fisher, *Religious Liberty in America: Political Safeguards* (Lawrence, KS: University of Kansas Press, 2002), 115–116.
11. *Bitterman v. Secretary of Defense*, 553 F. Supp. 719.
12. Michael Barone and Grant Ujifusa, *The Almanac of American Politics, 1988* (Washington, DC: *National Journal*, 1987), 821.
13. Telephone Interview with Rep. Steven Solarz, December 20, 2002.
14. Fisher, *Religious Liberty*, 117.
15. *Goldman v. Weinberger.*
16. Ibid.
17. Solarz interview, December 20, 2002.
18. Fisher *Religious Liberty*, 121.
19. Telephone interview with Nathan Lewin, January 13, 2003.
20. Telephone message from Nathan Lewin, January 23, 2003.

4

Forbidden Rituals

Yale Law School professor Stephen L. Carter wrote in *The Confirmation Mess*, "When a new justice is selected, what hangs in the balance is nothing so arcane as the correct approach to constitutional interpretation. What hangs in the balance, rather, is the list of rights to be protected, or unprotected, depending upon one's preferences."[1]

Decisions made by the Supreme Court are preeminently the result of who happens to be on the Court. While we sometimes imagine that interpretations of the basic rights enshrined in the Constitution are fixed and eternal, they are in fact subject to the views of whoever happens to constitute the majority on the Court at the time the right is in dispute. While justices generally follow the precedent of previous cases, established principles are sometimes overruled quite dramatically—for example, when the *Plessy v. Ferguson* decision permitting separate but equal segregated schools was overturned in *Brown v. Board of Education*. The addition or subtraction of a single justice from a majority can turn a 5–4 decision to a 4–5 decision in a short span of time. The free exercise clause and the compelling state interest test, already on shaky ground, would be reappraised by a court in transition.

In June 1986, Warren E. Burger announced that he would retire as chief justice. President Reagan quickly nominated Associate Justice William H. Rehnquist to succeed Burger. Rehnquist's elevation to the post of chief justice left a vacancy among the associate justices, and Reagan filled the vacancy with Antonin Scalia of the US Court of Appeals for the District of Columbia, the lone dissenting vote when the Circuit Court dismissed Capt. Simcha Goldman's appeal.

Associate justices who are nominated to be chief justice must be confirmed before they can take their new position, even though they are already members of the Court. Rehnquist's proposed elevation reignited some of the heated opposition to him that first surfaced in 1971 when President Richard M. Nixon nominated him as an associate justice. Much of the opposition centered on a memo Rehnquist had once written that criticized the Supreme Court's decision in *Brown v. Board of Education*, the case that held school segregation to be unconstitutional. He went even further and argued that the 1896 decision in *Plessy v. Ferguson* that upheld segregated public accommodations should be reaffirmed.[2] Despite lengthy and passionate opposition, Rehnquist was confirmed as chief justice by the Senate Judiciary Committee by a vote of 13–5 on August 14, 1986. Rehnquist's opponents dwelt principally on his criticism of the reasoning behind *Brown v. Board of Education* and other examples of what they considered racial bias and insensitivity. In Scalia's case, opponents turned their sights mainly on his apparent hostility to the legal reasoning that went into the 1973 Supreme Court decision in *Roe v. Wade*, which established that during the first trimester of pregnancy a woman had a virtually unlimited right to secure an abortion. Scalia, who proved an amiable witness, was recommended unanimously by the Judiciary Committee and confirmed by the Senate without so much as a single dissenting vote after only about five minutes of floor debate. The final vote on Rehnquist was preceded by five days of debate, and he received more negative votes than any other successful nominee.[3]

Questions relating to free exercise of religion did not constitute a major line of inquiry in either the Rehnquist or Scalia confirmation hearings. Neither the various religious groups nor their friends in Congress had any inkling that either Rehnquist or Scalia posed any threat to the broadest protection of the free exercise of religion. But it was not long after Rehnquist was installed in the center seat on the Court that a free exercise question was presented to the justices.

Prison Pieties

The case of *O'Lone v. Shabazz* had its origins in the Leesburg State Prison in Gloucester County in the southern part of New Jersey. Prison authorities there had forbidden inmates who were members of the Nation of Islam, an offshoot of orthodox Islam often referred to as the Black Muslims, to attend a Friday religious service. The prisoners contended that the warden and his staff had violated their free exercise rights. Prison officials maintained that policies set by the New Jersey Department of Corrections required that certain categories of prisoners deemed particularly dangerous, the Black Muslim plaintiffs among them, be prevented from working in certain prison buildings. The place where Muslim religious services were held was one of the buildings off-limits to dangerous inmates, including the plaintiffs.[4]

The view of the prison authorities was very similar to the position taken by the military in the Goldman case. Their argument, accepted by the US District Court that first heard the case in 1983, was that reasonable restrictions imposed on inmates in the interests of prison security did not violate the constitutional rights of the Muslims. The District Court also concluded that any action the prison officials could have taken to accommodate the religious needs of the inmates would create serious security problems at the facility.

The prisoners won the second round when the US Court of Appeals vacated the earlier decision and remanded the case to the District Court. A remand occurs when an appeals court finds that the trial court, in this case the US District Court in New Jersey that originally heard the case, committed an error important enough to have the case retried. If, for example, the trial court excluded evidence that the appeals court determines should have been admitted, the case is remanded, or sent back, to the trial court.

In the *O'Lone* case, the US Court of Appeals for the Third Circuit[5] sent the case back to the trial court with instructions to the judge that New Jersey prison officials should have been forced to prove that they could come up with no reasonable method to accommodate the inmates' religious needs that did not create genuine security problems inside the jail. The prison officials represented by Edward O'Lone, the administrator of the Leesburg prison, appealed the remand to the Supreme Court, which heard the case on March 24, 1987. In a strange twist of fate, the inmate who had originally filed suit, Ahmad Uthman Shabazz, died shortly before the case was heard by the Supreme Court.

The position taken by the majority of the Supreme Court, in a 5–4 decision written by Chief Justice Rehnquist, was a victory for the prison authorities. Joined by Justices Byron White, Lewis Powell, Sandra Day O'Connor, and the newly confirmed Antonin Scalia, Rehnquist held that the Court of Appeals had "erred in placing the burden on prison officials to disprove the availability of alternative methods of accommodating prisoners' religious rights." He added that the approach taken by the Appeals Court "fails to respect the deference the Constitution allows for the judgment of prison administrators." He also noted, using a phrase that comes close to the one used by other judges, that the policies adopted by the prison administrators that curtailed the Muslims' access to the prayer space had "a rational connection to the legitimate government interests of institutional order and security invoked to justify them. . . ."[6]

The *O'Lone* decision was a distinct echo of the *Goldman* case. On the face of it, an air force psychologist would seem to have little in common with a group of convicts, but the Court once again made the point that a distinctive institution with tightly structured rules in which order is paramount was entitled to invoke a compelling state (or governmental) interest to curtail the free exercise of religion by individuals within its jurisdiction. With *Goldman*, it was the military's need to preserve good order and military discipline that was inconsistent with an officer wearing a yarmulke. In *O'Lone*, it was the prison's need to maintain institutional order and security that trumped the Muslim prisoners' access to a particular building at a particular time.

In both these cases, the compelling state interest standard laid down in the *Sherbert* case against official infringements on the free exercise of religion was applied, and in both cases decisions were rendered adverse to those who felt their religious practices were in jeopardy.

Order and the Court

Could one have seen in these two free exercise cases any hint that the *Sherbert* standard was threatened? Not in any direct sense. But in a very broad way, the two decisions, although written by different justices, demonstrate a preference for order and authority over the religious practices of individuals, although it is certainly worth noting that both cases related to the free exercise of minority religions. As one observer noted:

> The Chief Justice's first opinion as Chief Justice on free exercise
> struck the note that preferred secular orderliness to recognition
> of the requirements of the spirit.[7]

Rehnquist could hardly be charged with being antireligious. Too many of his positions in other cases argue for the falsity of that proposition.[8] A fairer and more accurate characterization of Rehnquist's perspective is that social order was for him a value of considerable importance. Accordingly, he could with perfect consistency give preference to the disciplinary needs of the military and the prisons over religious expression and at the same time favor school prayer for its ability to have a calming effect on a disruptive class or to instill a sense of dignity and reverence in the young and obstreperous.

While at first glance it might seem something of a stretch, this predilection for conformity reveals "a striking but often overlooked pattern for the Rehnquist Court [which is] its consistency in deferring to government efforts to combat what often has been regarded as sinful behavior: nonmarital sex, drugs, and gambling.[9]

This passion for conventional behavior and for institutions of government strong enough to promote that conformity was noted by journalist Sidney Blumenthal, who wrote of what he deemed to be Rehnquist's affection for the power of the state, focusing on a 1980 speech in which Rehnquist argued that people were better off for having formed governments even though the governments themselves proved to be tyrannical. . . . It is better to endure the coercive force wielded by a government in which [ordinary citizens] have some say, rather than to risk the anarchy in which neither life, liberty, nor property are safe from the 'savage few.' "[10]

One aspect of the *O'Lone* case that signaled the possibility of future conflicts over free expression came from the many *amicus curiae* briefs filed by religious groups on behalf of the Black Muslim inmates and, on the other side, by state attorneys general. Altogether, five religious organizations, including the American Jewish Congress, the Catholic League for Religious and Civil Rights, the Christian Legal Society, and the American Civil Liberties Union, filed briefs for the inmates, and twenty-eight state attorneys general filed briefs in support of the New Jersey prison officials.

Holy Smoke

The case that would begin a lengthy and still unresolved clash between Congress and the federal courts was not about appropriate military headgear, taxes, schools, or the religious rights of people in America's prisons; it concerned *Lophophora williamsii Lemaire*, "a small, leafless, turnip-shaped cactus . . . considered sacred by a number of Indian tribes in North America, and has been used in religious ceremonies for centuries. Those who ingest the sacrament contend that . . . [it] is a spirit force that allows them to communicate with the Creator and obtain spiritual enlightenment."[11]

Peyote, the active ingredient in the plant, has a long and checkered history. Sometimes it was banned as a harmful drug; sometimes exceptions were made, by both state and federal law, allowing its use by Native Americans as part of religious rituals. Among the states, there is considerable variation in how the substance is treated. Twelve states and the federal government grant a limited exemption for religious use of peyote by restricting its use to members of the Native American Church, a Christian denomination with congregants from a number of tribes in North America. An additional seven states have a broader exemption that restricts its use to religious rituals but does not limit it to a single sect or denomination. Two dozen states classify peyote as a Schedule I drug and ban it even for religious purposes.[12]

Alfred Smith was a member of the Klamath Indian tribe and an adherent of the Native American Church. For eleven years, beginning in 1971, Smith worked as an alcohol-addiction counselor. In 1982, he got a job as a counselor with a group called ADAPT, Alcohol Drug Abuse Prevention and Treatment, a group founded in 1969 in Roseburg in Douglas County in southern Oregon. Earlier in Smith's life, he had been an alcoholic but he had been sober for twenty-five years before he came to work at ADAPT. ADAPT asked people who joined the program to pledge themselves to a program of total abstinence from drugs or alcohol.

Because he was an Indian and a recovering alcoholic, Smith was seen by the leadership of ADAPT as an ideal person to offer help to the many Indians in southern Oregon who abused alcohol. As a member of the Native American Church, with its sacramental rite of smoking peyote buds, Smith raised the suspicions of his superiors at ADAPT, and he was questioned by the executive director about the Native American Church and its use of the mind-altering drug in its ceremonies. He was then asked whether he had smoked peyote while on the ADAPT payroll. Smith denied that he had smoked peyote, but his boss put him on notice that he could be fired if he used it even for sacramental purposes.[13]

On March 2, 1984, Smith informed his supervisor that he would be attending a Native American Church meeting the following day. He was warned by his supervisor that if he smoked peyote during the ritual, he would be fired. Smith knew that this was no idle threat. Galen Black, a non-Indian coworker whom Smith had encouraged to join the church, had ingested peyote and been dismissed from his job at ADAPT. After the ceremony, upon acknowledging that he had smoked peyote, Alfred Smith was also fired.

Alfred Smith and Galen Black applied to the Oregon Department of Human Resources for unemployment benefits, but their applications were rejected because under Oregon law workers who are fired for misconduct are not eligible for unemployment compensation. Since even possession of peyote was a crime in Oregon, smoking it would seem to be a clear case of misconduct. The two appealed the denial to the Oregon Court of Appeals, which held that they had been improperly denied benefits. The court added:

> The Department of Human Resources had placed a burden on the right to free exercise of religion of both men, and in such a case, the state must demonstrate that the limitation it placed on free exercise was the least restrictive means of meeting a compelling state interest.[14]

The judge who wrote the opinion on behalf of the Appeals Court's majority stated that the precedent set by the US Supreme Court in *Sherbert v. Verner* was the controlling one and that the "compelling state interest" standard applied. The appeals court, balancing Smith's and Black's right to free exercise against the state's argument that the men's claims represented undeserving raids on the state's unemployment compensation fund, found the state's interests not compelling.

At this point, Dave Frohnmeyer, the attorney general of Oregon, one of the attorneys general who had filed the *amicus curiae* brief in the O'Lone case on behalf of his state, became involved in the peyote case. The issue was fairly straightforward. He told Carolyn Long in an interview:

> We saw it almost completely as a drug case. We knew there was a First Amendment issue related to it, because it was a religious practice . . . but the notion that someone can affirmatively claim . . . money from taxes that are coercively extracted from

other people, for engaging in activity which for someone not of that religion would actually violate criminal law seemed almost nonsensical.[15]

Until this point, the state had based its case on what it charged was the men's unwarranted raid on the taxpayer-supported state unemployment compensation fund, that depleting the fund with unjustified claims would jeopardize the entire system of benefits, and that the preservation of that fund was the compelling state interest.[16]

Frohnmeyer decided to take the case to the state's highest court, the Oregon Supreme Court. The case was argued on April 1, 1986, with the state's solicitor general presenting the case that the appeals court decision be reversed and an attorney for Oregon Legal Services, representing Smith and Black, arguing that it be upheld. The Oregon Supreme Court took almost three months to make the decision, and handed it down on June 24, 1986.

It was a complicated decision because the denial of unemployment benefits that followed the dismissal of Smith and Black was subjected to two separate constitutional tests—the US Constitution and the constitution of the State of Oregon. The Oregon justices rejected the arguments by the lawyer for Smith and Black that the denial of benefits violated the Oregon state constitution's protection of freedom of worship. It then affirmed the Court of Appeals decision to reinstate the benefits to the two men by agreeing with the lower court that their free exercise rights under the US Constitution had been violated by the Employment Commission.

Making reference to *Sherbert v. Verner,* as the Appeals Court had done, the Oregon Supreme Court said that whenever a state places a burden on the free exercise of religion, it must prove that this burden is the least restrictive means of achieving a compelling state interest. They applied the so-called "balancing test."

The basis of the state's argument, that the integrity of its unemployment compensation fund was being undermined by false claims, was not sufficiently compelling to deny the two men their

benefits. The Oregon Supreme Court reasoned that the Employment Division's denial of benefits to Smith and Black for misconduct was not with the purpose of enforcing the criminal law—
which might have been a compelling state interest—but with preserving the integrity of the unemployment fund—which, in the
eyes of the court, was not compelling enough to burden the free
exercise of religion.[17] On the same day that Smith's case was decided, Black's was also, and with the same result, a victory for
the dismissed workers and the reinstatement of their benefits.

After failing to get the Oregon Supreme Court to reconsider
its decision, Attorney General Frohnmeyer resolved to take the
case to the US Supreme Court. He applied to the Court for a writ
of *certiorari*. This writ is the principal means by which cases are
accepted by the Court. The Employment Division, on whose behalf Frohnmeyer sought the writ, was the petitioner. The opposing parties, Smith and Black, who had won the case before the
Oregon Supreme Court, were the respondents. *Certiorari*, or
"cert" as it is called by attorneys who plead before the Supreme
Court, is granted in only about 5 percent of all cases. Whether
or not the Supreme Court will grant *certiorari* is impossible to
predict, except to note that if enough justices think a case is important, they will grant the writ.

In its first appearance at the US Supreme Court, the Oregon
peyote case produced a result that was not entirely satisfying to
either side. The case was argued before the US Supreme Court
on December 8, 1987, and five months later, on April 27, 1988,
Justice John Paul Stevens delivered the opinion of the Court. It
called for the decision of the Oregon Supreme Court to be vacated
and for the case to be remanded to that court. To vacate an order
is to declare it null and void. To remand, as we have said, is to
send the case back to the court from which the appeal was taken.

What was it that caused the justices of the Supreme Court
to void the decision of the Oregon Supreme Court? Essentially,
it came down to this: It was unclear to the US Supreme Court
justices whether the law of Oregon which made possession of

peyote a Class B felony also made the use of the drug for religious purposes illegal. The Oregon Supreme Court had not addressed this issue, because, as noted above, they had determined that this case was not about drug laws, but about unemployment fund policies. The United States Supreme Court believed that Oregon drug law was relevant and therefore needed the Oregon court to make a determination as to whether peyote was covered by the Oregon law. Justice Stevens observed:

> A substantial number of jurisdictions have exempted the use of peyote in religious ceremonies from legislative prohibitions against the use and possession of controlled substances. If Oregon is one of those States, respondents' [Smith and Black] conduct may well be entitled to constitutional protection.

One passage in the Supreme Court's opinion raised the possibility that its view of Smith's and Black's situation might be viewed differently from that of Adell Sherbert and more like that of the Utah polygamist George Reynolds:

> The results we reached in *Sherbert* . . . might well have been different if the employees had been discharged for engaging in criminal conduct. We have held that bigamy is forbidden, even when the practice is dictated by sincere religious convictions. [They make reference here to *U.S. v. Reynolds;* see pp. 16–17.] If a bigamist may be sent to jail despite the religious motivation for his misconduct, surely a State may refuse to pay unemployment compensation to a marriage counselor who was discharged because he or she entered into a bigamous relationship. *The protection that the First Amendment provides to legitimate claims to free exercise of religion . . . does not extend to conduct that a State has validly proscribed* (emphasis added).[18]

Responding to the remand, the Oregon Supreme Court on October 18, 1988, glossed over the US Supreme Court's query about whether or not the use of peyote in a religious ceremony was a violation of Oregon's criminal law, although they did note that the statute provided no exceptions to the general ban on the substance. Despite the lack of any exception in the law, the Oregon Supreme Court concluded that an outright prohibition against the use of peyote in a religious ceremony violated Smith's and Black's free exercise rights under the First Amendment to the Constitution. In support of its decision, the Oregon Supreme Court cited three acts of Congress from the 1960s and 1970s that specifically exempted peyote from the list of controlled substances when it was used in the religious rituals of the Native American Church. They kicked the case back to the State Employment Division and told them to grant the two men their unemployment compensation.

As we learned in the case of *Cantwell v. Connecticut*, the Supreme Court had deemed the free exercise clause applicable to the actions of states by reason of its having been incorporated into the Fourteenth Amendment, and the action by a state agency, in this case the employment board, was seen by the Oregon court as an unconstitutional encroachment.

Attorney General Frohnmeyer might at that point have simply run up the white flag. Persisting by seeking another writ of *certiorari* might be seen as hostile to Native Americans, but Frohnmeyer evidently saw the case as more of a law-enforcement problem than one of First Amendment rights. According to one observer, he was concerned that a religious exception to the state's drug laws might trigger numerous claims by people who simply wanted access to illegal drugs and would cite the *Smith* and *Black* cases in support.[19] Thus, he filed his second *certiorari* petition to the US Supreme Court on January 17, 1989.

A main point in Frohnmeyer's plea for *certiorari* was that the Oregon Supreme Court had not made a truly independent assessment of the case but had relied instead on interpretations of the US Constitution by Congress. He further argued that the state of Oregon had a legitimate interest in protecting the public from dangerous drugs.

By a 5–4 vote, on March 20, 1989, the Court granted *certiorari*.[20] Between the two appearances of the Oregon peyote cases before the US Supreme Court, an event occurred that seemed to make the entire controversy moot. ADAPT, the drug counseling program that had fired Smith and Black, signed a consent decree with the federal government stipulating that ritual use of peyote by members of the native American Church would no longer be cause for dismissal. Smith and Black were awarded back pay and were guaranteed they would not have to reimburse the state for their benefits they had received in the event that the US Supreme Court reversed the decision of the Oregon Supreme Court.[21]

When Frohnmeyer argued the case before the US Supreme Court, he did not challenge the compelling state interest test set forth in *Sherbert v. Verner*.

He recommended that the Court use the same balancing test it employed over the last several decades when it evaluated religious requests for exemptions to state or federal laws; the state's interest must be balanced against the individual's religious interest, and "religious conduct must give way to regulations that serve public interests of compelling importance."[22]

Based upon the standard set forth in the *Sherbert* case, then, Attorney General David Frohnmeyer could take comfort in the fact that he had made a persuasive case that placing Oregon's need to curb the use of dangerous drugs by all Oregonians on one side of a balance scale and the encroachment of Al Smith's and Galen Black's use of peyote in a religious ceremony on the other, the justices would see the state's needs as compelling. But when the US Supreme Court handed down its decision on April 17, 1990, Frohnmeyer got far more from the justices than he had asked for. The decision in *Employment Division, Department of Human Resources of Oregon, et al. v. Smith et al.* would lead to a monumental constitutional clash between the US Supreme Court and the US Congress that would rank among the most contentious and prolonged in modern history.

Notes

1. Carter, *The Confirmation Mess*, 129.
2. Tinsley E. Yarborough, *The Rehnquist Court and the Constitution* (New York: Oxford University Press, 2000), 1–4.
3. Ibid., 11–14.
4. *O'Lone v. Shabazz* 482 U.S. 342 (1987).
5. The Third Circuit consists of the states of Pennsylvania, New Jersey, Delaware, and the Virgin Islands.
6. *O'Lone v. Shabazz*, 1.
7. John T. Noonan, Jr., "The First Freedom and the Rehnquist Court," in Martin H. Belsky, ed., *The Rehnquist Court* (New York: Oxford University Press, 2002), 74.
8. See *Wallace v. Jaffree* 472 U.S. 38 (1985), in which the Supreme Court struck down a 1978 Alabama law authorizing school boards to provide a minute of silence or meditation, along with two subsequent laws providing for a period of "meditation or voluntary prayer" and for teachers to lead "willing students" in prayers. Rehnquist wrote one of three dissents, and his was the most forceful, offering a novel view of the doctrine of the separation of church and state.
9. Erwin Chermerinsky, "The Constitutional Jurisprudence of the Rehnquist Court," in Belsky, ed., *The Rehnquist Court*, 198. While this observation was made more than ten years after the *O'Lone* decision, it captures a pattern that was set very early in Rehnquist's tenure as chief justice.
10. Quoted in Sidney Blumenthal, *Our Long National Daydream* (New York: Harper & Row, 1988), 186.
11. Carolyn Long, *Religious Freedom and Indian Rights*, 4. (Lawrence, KS: University Press of Kansas, 2000), 4.
12. Ibid., 17.
13. Ibid., 36–41.
14. Louis Fisher, *Religious Liberty in America*, 183–185; and Carolyn N. Long, "Congress, the Court, and Religious Liberty: The Case of Employment Division of Oregon v. Smith," in Colton C. Campbell and John F. Stack, Jr., eds., *Congress Confronts the Court* (Lanham, MD: Rowman & Littlefield, 2001), 80–82.
15. Long, *Religious Freedom and Indian Rights*, 93–94.
16. Ibid.
17. *Employment Division, Department of Human Resources of Oregon, et al. v. Smith et al.* 494 US 872 (1990).
18. Ibid.
19. Long, *Religious Freedom and Indian Rights*, 153.

20. The five who voted to grant *certiorari* were Chief Justice Rehnquist and Associate Justices Stevens, O'Connor, Scalia, and White; the four opposed were Associate Justices Brennan, Marshall, Blackmun, and Kennedy.
21. Louis Fisher, *Religious Liberty in America*, 185–186.
22. Long, *Religious Freedom and Indian Rights*, 157.

5

Judicial Challenge and Congressional Response

O n April 17, 1990, the United States Supreme Court handed down its decision in the case of *Employment Division, Department of Human Resources of Oregon, et al. v. Smith et al.* Attorney Nathan Lewin, who had represented Captain Simcha Goldman in the yarmulke case and had been instrumental in lobbying to get Congress to nullify the *Goldman* ruling, was in Los Angeles on business. He read about the decision in the *Los Angeles Times* and was thunderstruck by the dramatic and sweeping decision of the Court majority and the accompanying opinion written by Associate Justice Antonin Scalia.

Lewin had assumed that the decision would make only marginal changes in the existing law. He recalls:

> I remember thinking at the time, Gee, this is going to be a decision where the Court's going to narrow *Sherbert v. Verner* and all of those other compensation cases, but it will do so only in the context of saying that it's different when there's criminal action involved. I never anticipated until the Court came out with its decision that they would do what they did.[1]

Other reactions to the decision were characterized less as surprise than as outrage. Professor Michael McConnell of the University of Chicago Law School called the decision "one of the clearest reversals of important constitutional precedent in a decade." He warned that the decision "could affect cases in which Moslem schoolchildren seek time during school to engage in daily prayers or Jewish prisoners assert that they are entitled to kosher meals."[2]

Steven Shapiro of the American Civil Liberties Union, which had filed an *amicus curiae* brief on behalf of Al Smith and the members of the Native American Church, was even more apocalyptic in his forecast of what would result from the decision.

> The ruling significantly erodes the protection for religious freedom. Drawing a parallel to the period in which the manufacture and sale of alcohol was banned in the United States, he speculated that as a result of the *Smith* decision, it would have been criminal to use communion wine in a Catholic Church during Prohibition.[3]

What had the Court done to engender such expressions of surprise and consternation? Justice Scalia and five other justices did several things. First off, they rejected the claims of Native Americans that Oregon's law banning the use of peyote under all circumstances violated their free exercise of religion. Second, they said that the purpose of the Oregon law was not to target any religion; the Oregon statute was "a law of general applicability" that prohibited the use of peyote by all people in Oregon because it was a narcotic. Indians were not being singled out. Scalia in his opinion went on to say that the First Amendment does not forbid the states to pass laws of general applicability that have incidental impact on religious practice. But the part of the decision that caused the greatest consternation among religious groups and civil libertarians was Scalia's response to the claim by the Native Americans that even those incidental burdens imposed on religious groups by laws that are not directed at religion must be subjected to the compelling state interest test laid down in 1963 in *Sherbert v. Verner.*

To that argument, Scalia said that, aside from compensation cases (typically involving people dismissed from jobs and denied unemployment benefits), the Court had not, in recent years, applied the compelling-state-interest test. He cited the *Goldman* case as one example of the Court's refraining from using the test. Then he added, "Even if we were inclined to breathe into *Sherbert* some life beyond the unemployment compensation field, we would not apply it to require exemptions from a generally applicable criminal law." Then, to add further emphasis, Scalia wrote:

> The government's ability to enforce generally applicable prohibitions of socially harmful conduct . . . cannot depend upon measuring the effects of governmental action on a religious objector's spiritual development. To make an individual's obligation to obey a law contingent upon the law's coincidence with his religious beliefs except where the state's interest is "compelling"—permitting him, by virtue of his beliefs, "to become a law unto himself"—contradicts both constitutional tradition and common sense.[4]

The Court, had it chosen to do so, could have denied the free exercise claims of Smith and Black without scrapping the compelling state interest test. They could simply have found that Oregon did, in fact, have a compelling state interest in suppressing drug use and stopped there, leaving the *Sherbert* test intact. In discarding the test, in the words of one observer,

> The *Smith* ruling granted state governments broad powers over religious practices. . . . The ruling [was] highly troublesome to many constitutional scholars because it seems to offer minority religions little protection from state legislative enactments that infringe on their religious practices.[5]

While the criticism of the decision greatly outweighed the praise, Scalia's opinion was not without its defenders. As one wrote, "Scalia wisely . . . held in *Smith* that 'an individual's religious beliefs do not excuse him from compliance with an otherwise valid law prohibiting conduct that the state is free to regulate.' "[6]

On April 19, 1990, the day after the *Smith* decision was handed down, Morton Halperin, the head of the Washington DC office of the American Civil Liberties Union, appeared at room 1536 of the Longworth House Office Building, the suite of Rep. Steven Solarz. In his hand was a copy of the *Smith* decision. The two men had collaborated to prevail on Congress to reverse by legislation the decision in *Goldman,* and Halperin was clearly upset. "Steve," he said, "you've got to do something about this." Solarz handed the opinion to David Lachmann, an attorney on the staff of the House Judiciary Committee, and told him to take it home and read it. As Lachmann recalls, "I took it home and read it. I actually read it with my wife, who had written a law review article on a related topic, and our eyes kept getting bigger and bigger as we read this thing."[7]

Echoing Nathan Lewin's surprise, Lachmann recalled, "It was particularly stunning because nobody saw it coming." The surprise, according to Lachmann, came from the fact that the majority opinion of the Court had gone well beyond what the State of Oregon had argued in defense of its position. Oregon, he emphasized, had never asked the Court to scrap the compelling-state-interest standard, or even ask that it be reviewed. "And then along comes this decision," said Lachmann. "It was really one of the more monumental pieces of judicial sophistry that any of us had ever seen."[8]

The question of what was to be done to challenge the Court was the subject of a dinner conversation between Halperin and Solarz. In the course of the dinner Halperin urged Solarz to introduce legislation that would, in effect, restore by legislation the compelling-state-interest test.

Congress Strikes Back

Having succeeded in neutralizing the Supreme Court's decision in the *Goldman* case, Solarz, Halperin, and Lewin sought to pull off the same feat with the *Smith* decision. It appeared at the time that their task might be even easier because of several factors, particularly because word of the *Smith* decision had spread quickly throughout the religious community and united a broad coalition of members of Congress, who saw the restoration of the *Sherbert* standard as a popular issue. On July 26, 1990, Rep. Solarz introduced the Religious Freedom Restoration Act of 1990.

The name given to a bill is no small matter, and the member who introduces the bill, its sponsor, usually chooses a lofty or inspiring title. "An attractive title, such as the Freedom of Information Act or the American Dream Restoration Act, could garner a bill useful media attention."[9]

Even more useful politically in this title was the large list of cosponsors and the ideological breadth it represented. Few members of Congress would not want to be associated with a bill entitled the "Religious Freedom Restoration Act." Cosponsorship is a common practice in Congress; invitations to join bills as cosponsors arrive daily in congressional offices in the form of "Dear Colleague" letters. David Mayhew writes of members of the Senate who "ostentatiously line up as cosponsors of measures—an activity that may attract more attention than . . . voting itself." He quotes a senator on the subject of why so many of his colleagues signed on as cosponsors of a bill to block trade concessions to the Soviet Union until they permitted the emigration of Jews. The senator responded, "Because there is no political advantage in not signing. If you do sign, you don't offend anyone. If you don't sign, you might offend some Jews in your state."[10]

There were ninety-nine cosponsors for the Religious Freedom Restoration Act; they ran the ideological gamut from the most liberal Democrats such as Barney Frank of Massachusetts to the ultraconservative Robert K. Dornan of California. The bill itself was straightforward:

> It prohibited any government authority from restricting anyone's free exercise of religion unless "the restriction is in the form of a law of general applicability that does not target religion, and the government authority proves that the restriction is the least restrictive way to further a compelling government interest."[11]

A coalition of interest groups had formed to push the legislation in Congress, calling itself the "Coalition for Religious Freedom." Solarz recalls that "Mort [Halperin of the ACLU] and others put together one of the most eclectic coalitions in the history of American politics, ranging from the American Baptist Convention to the American Civil Liberties Union."[12]

A common response to what is perceived as an unjust situation is "There ought to be a law." Most Americans unfamiliar with the Constitution no doubt believe that Congress can pass a law on virtually any subject. Even those who have studied the Constitution often note the words of Article I, that Congress has the authority "make all laws necessary and proper," and overlook the next clause, which limits that authority to laws "carrying into execution" the detailed list of specific powers in the previous eighteen paragraphs, such as the power to tax and spend and the power to declare war.

In the case of Congress's response to the *Goldman* case, the authority of Congress to undo the Court decision was clear. It was found in the power specified in Article I "To make Rules for the Government and Regulation of the land and naval forces." Congress was on unassailable ground in that confrontation with the Court. Not so clear was the authority of Congress to counteract *Smith*.

"by appropriate legislation"

The Coalition for Religious Freedom, in collaboration with Solarz and his staff, determined that the constitutional authority they needed to counteract the *Smith* decision could be found in Section 5 of the Fourteenth Amendment. In Chapters 1 and 2, we first encountered this monumental post–Civil War amendment in terms of the lengthy period required to incorporate all of its provisions so that they restrained the states fully as much as the federal government against encroachments on basic freedoms. We also considered it briefly in discussing the limitations that Congress can impose on the Supreme Court. The critical passage in the Fourteenth Amendment is Section 5, which gives to Congress the "power to enforce, by appropriate legislation, the provision of this article."

A series of modern decisions by the Supreme Court provided Solarz and the coalition members a reasonable expectation that their reinstatement of the *Sherbert* standard might stand up to scrutiny by the justices. Beginning in 1964 with the major civil rights legislation of that year, the Court had upheld Congress's Section 5 powers to broaden civil rights protection for individuals beyond that which the Court had granted. Because free exercise of religion had been incorporated by the *Cantwell* case and its protections made applicable to the states, the coalition strategists believed they were on firm constitutional grounds.[13]

> The line of decisions unquestionably established Congress's right to use its [Section 5] enforcement authority to adopt remedial and preventative legislation to protect constitutional rights against abuses by state and local governments. *However, Congress's right to modify the Court's substantive constitutional interpretations was less than clear* [emphasis added].[14]

In the venerable practice on Capitol Hill of reducing cumbersome titles to shorthand, the Religious Freedom Restoration Act was quickly reduced to an awkward acronym, RFRA, usually pronounced "Rifra." Introduced just before Congress's August recess in 1990, the bill was referred to the Subcommittee on Constitutional Rights of the House Judiciary Committee just before members went on their summer break. The chairman of the subcommittee was Rep. Don Edwards [D-CA], one of most liberal members of the House. But the ecumenical nature of RFRA, from both a religious and political standpoint, was clear from the fact that when hearings began on September 27, 1990, the two members who testified before Edwards's committee were the left-leaning Solarz and Rep. Lamar Smith, a conservative Republican Christian Scientist from San Antonio, Texas.

Smith was a member of the committee but Solarz was not. Normally, a legislator is in a better position to advance legislation if he or she is a member of the committee that has jurisdiction over the bill, but Solarz

> . . . was recognized as a leader on these issues, so the fact that he showed up for this bill and we had a ready-made coalition surprised nobody. When Steve Solarz and every religious group in America suddenly turned up on Edwards' doorstep and said, '*Smith* is a catastrophe for religious liberty in America, and you've got to do something about it,' this is not where people were saying why the hell is he here. It made sense to everybody.[15]

Time had run out on RFRA in the 101st Congress, however. The House adjourned so that members could return to their districts for the 1990 congressional elections. Because the bill had not progressed very far in the 101st Congress, it died in subcommittee, but it came roaring back in the 102nd Congress when Solarz reintroduced it under a new bill number, H.R. 2797, on June 26, 1991. This time the cosponsors numbered 195.[16]

Another difference between 1990 and 1991 is that in the latter year, there was a companion bill introduced in the Senate. Had the sponsors of RFRA succeeded in the House, their task would still have been incomplete without passage in the Senate. In the Senate the advocates of RFRA found a powerful sponsor, Senator Edward M. Kennedy [D-MA], the second most senior Democrat on the Judiciary Committee, which, like its counterpart in the House, took jurisdiction over the bill. Also encouraging to backers of the bill were the twenty-six cosponsors who lent their support. As in the House the previous year, the list of Senate cosponsors was impressive in its breadth, from staunch liberals such as Kennedy and Minnesota Democrat Paul Wellstone to some of the most conservative Republicans, such as Utah's Orrin Hatch and Idaho's Larry Craig, who had just been elected to the Senate in 1990, having come from the House, where he was a cosponsor of the House version of RFRA.

The hearings held in the Senate on September 18, 1992, were presided over by Senator Kennedy in the absence of the chairman, Senator Joseph Biden of Delaware. Inasmuch as Kennedy and the second-ranking Republican on the Judiciary Committee were both strongly in favor of RFRA, the witness list was tilted strongly in the direction of the legislation. Committee chairmen have great latitude in how and when hearings are conducted. Witness lists can be loaded to favor one side or the other, and the sequence in which witnesses appear can be important in making the case for the bill or undercutting it. In the case of S.2969, the hearing that was held on Friday, September 18, 1992, was overwhelmingly pro-RFRA. Of the eleven witnesses who appeared, only one, former Reagan Administration deputy attorney general and conservative legal scholar Bruce Fein, made a comprehensive attack on the bill. Fein's argument was based primarily on federalism. "I don't think," Fein told the committee, "that the Supreme Court has ever accepted the idea that Congress may invade state sovereignty simply because a majority may disagree with a Supreme Court interpretation of a constitutional right." Fein added—prophetically, as it turned out—"I am very dubious that even given the greatest latitude to some of the previous Supreme Court decisions . . . that this court would uphold congressional power under Section 5 of the Fourteenth Amendment. . . ."[17]

Two witnesses found fault with one particular aspect of the bill, although they approved of the idea of restoring the *Sherbert* standard. These two witnesses, Mark E. Chopko, general counsel to the United States Catholic Conference, and James Bopp, Jr., general counsel to the National Right to Life Committee, wanted an amendment to the bill, a provision, as Bopp's statement said, "excluding a claim to a right to an abortion under RFRA."[18]

This is not an easy argument to follow. Basically, the two anti-abortion witnesses who supported RFRA only on the condition that the amendment be added were concerned that a woman seeking to end her pregnancy could claim that abortion was permitted by her religion and invoke RFRA to support that claim. At the time there was a feeling among both pro-life and pro-choice advocates that the Supreme Court might overturn the 1973 decision in *Roe v. Wade* legalizing abortion in the first three months of pregnancy. If *Roe* were overturned, the argument went, women could get legal support for abortion with RFRA by claiming that their religions allowed abortions. The argument over a religious right to an abortion succeeded in sinking the second effort by Congress to counteract the *Smith* decision, and its supporters had to wait until the first session of the 103rd Congress, which convened in January 1993.

Third Time's the Charm

RFRA was back for the 103rd Congress, but Steven Solarz was not. In March 1992, a scandal enveloped the House of Representatives; It was revealed that a number of House members had enjoyed what amounted to overdraft privileges on their checking accounts in a bank used by members. This enabled congressmen and congresswomen to write checks even if the balances in their accounts were insufficient to cover the amount of the check. Rep. Solarz wrote 743 of these checks. Worse still for Solarz, his strongest ally in the New York legislature, Assembly Speaker Mel Miller, was forced from office. This meant that the protection from unfavorable redistricting that Solarz had once enjoyed was taken away, and he was compelled to run against another Democrat, Rep. Ted Weiss. Solarz's old district had been wholly in Brooklyn. The new district included parts of Manhattan whose voters were less friendly to him. He declined to run against Weiss and, instead, ran in a largely Latino district and was defeated.

The new House sponsor of RFRA was Rep. (now Senator) Charles E. Schumer. The number of cosponsors dipped to 170, but in the Senate the number of sponsors rose to sixty when Senator Kennedy introduced it on March 11, 1993. The number sixty is particularly significant, because it is the number of senators required to invoke cloture, the step that terminates debate and allows a vote to take place. Unlike the House, where a simple majority enables a vote to proceed, in the Senate, unless the majority leader can get the unanimous consent of his colleagues to proceed to a vote or convince sixty of them to vote to end debate that is obstructing a vote, familiarly known as a filibuster, approval of the bill is impossible. The sixty cosponsors who had pledged to support RFRA were not a guarantee of passage, but they were a highly auspicious sign.

The question of constitutionality raised in the hearings by Bruce Fein did not halt the progress of RFRA. Amendments to the bill in the Senate were turned back easily, and although further consideration of the bill was postponed in the Senate at the end of October, the bill became law on November 16, 1993, as Public Law No. 103-141 when it was signed by President Bill Clinton.

Cynical observers of Congress say that the weakest argument you can make to a senator or House member to convince him or her to vote against a popular piece of legislation is that the bill is unconstitutional. The logic according to the cynics runs this way: Why vote against a popular bill that could be unconstitutional if, by voting for it, you get the approval of your voters? And what's the worst that could happen? The Supreme Court will overturn it, so no constitutional harm will be done, and you will have retained the favor of your constituents for supporting a popular bill. To be clear, it is not generally suggested that this devious reasoning played a prominent role in the overwhelming support that the Religious Freedom Restoration Act enjoyed when it became law. The backers of the bill no doubt believed that they enjoyed a constitutional warrant by the terms of Section 5 of the Fourteenth Amendment to broaden the definition of free exercise to prevent states from infringing on the free exercise of religion without extraordinary reasons for doing so.

They apparently did not grasp that enactment of RFRA might be understood by the United States Supreme Court as a usurpation by the House and Senate of the Court's power to interpret the Constitution. "We had viewed this very much as an exercise of our Section 5 powers under the Fourteenth Amendment," commented House Judiciary Committee staffer David Lachmann. "What we didn't see was the Supreme Court thinking that Congress had told them, 'Screw you, we're going to interpret the Constitution.'"[19]

Lawrence Baum has observed that unlike Congress, a generalist institution whose laws span a vast area of public policy from welfare to energy to military policy, the Supreme Court is a specialist institution. What the Supreme Court specializes in is, of course, the Constitution, and therefore such issues as First Amendment questions relating to the free exercise of religion. Congress rarely legislates in the area of basic rights—the reason, perhaps, that the Supreme Court viewed the Religious Freedom Restoration Act as a raid on its own turf.[20]

Notes

1. Telephone interview with Nathan Lewin, March 17, 2003.
2. Ruth Marcus, "Court: States Can Ban Peyote in Rites," *Washington Post*, April 18, 1990.
3. Ibid.
4. *Employment Division, Department of Human Resources of Oregon et al. v. Smith, et al.* 494 US 872 (1990).
5. Derek Davis, *Original Intent* (Buffalo, NY.: Prometheus Books, 1991), 124–125.
6. Stephen B. Presser, *Recapturing the Constitution* (Washington, DC: Henry Regnery, 1994), 155.
7. Telephone interview with David Lachmann, Minority Professional Staff Member, House Committee on the Judiciary, May 2, 2003.
8. Ibid.
9. Walter J. Oleszek, *Congressional Procedures and the Policy Process*, 5th ed. (Washington DC: CQ Press, 2001). Being associated with such felicitously named bills assists members of Congress in what David R. Mayhew has called "position-taking," "the public enunciation of a judgmental statement on anything likely to be of interest to political actors." See David R. Mayhew, *Congress: The Electoral Connection* (New Haven, CT: Yale University Press, 1974), 61–62.
10. Quoted in Mayhew, *Congress*, 64.
11. U.S. Congress. House Committee on the Judiciary. 1990. *Religious Freedom Restoration* Act of 1990. 101st Cong., 2nd sess. 27 July.
12. Telephone interview with Rep. Steven Solarz, March 21, 2003.
13. Carolyn N. Long, "Congress, The Court, and Religious Liberty," 84–85.
14. Ibid.

15. Telephone interview with David Lachmann, May 2, 2003.

16. The designation H.R. indicates that the legislation was a bill rather than a joint resolution, which would have been called H.J. Res. Both require the approval of both houses to become law, but the joint resolution is usually reserved for constitutional amendments. It is sometimes the case that bills that have failed to pass a previous congress retain their bill number. That was not the case with RFRA, which was first introduced as H.R. 5377.

17. U.S. Congress. Senate. Committee on the Judiciary. *A Bill to Protect the Free Exercise of Religion. Hearing before the Committee on the Judiciary* on S. 2969, 102nd Congress, 2nd sess. 1992.

18. Ibid.

19. Lachmann interview, May 2, 2003.

20. Lawrence Baum, *The Supreme Court*, 7th ed. (Washington DC: CQ Press, 2001), 193–94.

6

Priests and Preservationists

A s we have seen in previous chapters, constitutional issues of the most towering importance often arise from the most unremarkable controversies involving the most ordinary people. First there was William Marbury and his relentless quest for the hardly lofty post of justice of the peace. Then there was George Reynolds, the clerk who offered himself up for prosecution to test the constitutionality of the federal antipolygamy law. There were the Cantwells, doggedly proselytizing in the streets of New Haven with their tracts and windup record player, and of course, Adell Sherbert, the millhand who refused to work on her Sabbath. Equally obscure both before and after their constitutional debut were the peyote-smoking Indian, Al Smith, and his friend Galen Black. Of all the names in these cases, only James Madison, the defendant in the case that produced judicial review, would be recognized were it not for the centrality of these cases to the development of constitutional law.

Our focus in this book is on the constitutional right to the free exercise of religion. Because the United States has served for its entire existence as a refuge for those persecuted for their religion, Americans regard themselves as tolerant people. Yet, as the previous cases have shown, beliefs and practices that are deemed to be out of the mainstream are disproportionately involved in free exercise litigation. Adherents to these faiths and sects are often outsiders, distinct from the bulk of the population by their attire, their mode of prayer, and their theological beliefs that are exotic in the eyes of the majority.

While it is often the customs and practices of minority religious groups that find their way to the docket of the Supreme Court, major religions can also become ensnared in these controversies. One case arose in a small town nestled in the Texas Hill Country with a name that most outsiders mispronounce. In that unlikely locale a controversy developed, not over unconventional forms of worship or exotic sacraments, but out of a dispute over zoning. This normally undramatic issue would provide the United States Supreme Court with the pretext to retaliate against the United States Congress for its passage of the Religious Freedom Restoration Act.

"Upon This Rock I Will Build My Church"

The city of Boerne, Texas, lies sixteen miles north of San Antonio. Adjacent to Interstate 10, the town has become a popular place to settle for retirees and people who work in San Antonio and prefer the rugged limestone terrain of the Hill Country to the polished suburbs that ring the city. Boerne (pronounced "Bernie") was settled in the mid-nineteenth century by German immigrants, many of whom had fled Germany after the failed revolution of 1848. Some were devout Catholics, but others rejected the authority of the Church. From the very beginning of the town, there was a history of tension between believers and those who preferred reason to revelation.

One feature that makes Boerne an especially appealing place to live is the historic district, which includes most of downtown Boerne. The old limestone buildings conjure up memories of frontier Texas. One building is especially evocative of this early period, even though it is not in the heart of the downtown district—the Catholic Church of St. Peter the Apostle, built in 1923 on the site of a much older mission church. The historic charm of this and other structures led the city in 1985 to create the Historic Landmark Commission to preserve the town's historic buildings, and in 1987, Patrick Heath, the town's newly elected mayor, appointed the members of the commission.

In mid-1990, about the same time that the Supreme Court was handing down its decision in the Oregon peyote case, St. Peter's acquired a new priest, the Rev. Tony Cummins, who had previously served at a church in San Antonio. A dynamic and intense man, Father Tony quickly determined that the modest size of the sanctuary could no longer accommodate a congregation that was growing, and in 1991 he requested that Archbishop Patrick F. Flores of the Diocese of San Antonio, whose jurisdiction included the city of Boerne, grant permission for the church to be enlarged. The Archbishop gave his approval and architectural firms were interviewed. The winning design was produced by Gregory Davis, who proceeded to hold a series of meetings with members of the community to determine if the old church, or at least most of it, could be preserved.[1]

In December of 1991, after lengthy public hearings, the city added to the zoning map of Boerne an overlay that set the boundaries of the historic district. The historic district which, ironically, took the shape of a cross, included the church of St. Peter the Apostle. The new ordinance required owners of buildings within the historic district to apply for a certificate of appropriateness if they wished to change the exterior of any building, whether or not it had historic significance. Even a change in the exterior color of a building required approval. If a change was denied, the building owner had the right to appeal the zoning board's decision to the city council. Mayor Heath conceded:

> The rules are fairly stringent. Our rationale is that it's not just historic structures that need to be saved and maintained, it is the context, where they're sitting, and the district itself. It's not intrusive. It doesn't tell anyone what you can or can't do inside the building, it's just what's visible from a public way.[2]

Throughout 1992, architect Greg Davis, working with the congregation, went through a consensus-building process and developed a design that called for tearing down two-thirds of the building but preserving the entire facade, including the two distinctive towers. As Davis recalls, "We were building a building for about 700, which was smaller than they really wanted but all that they could afford financially. So we went to the city manager and the city staff engineer, not the city council, and they said, 'Boy, it looks great, no problem,'"[3] and he was told to go ahead with the drawings for the changes to the church. As Davis was preparing the drawings for presentation, an event was taking place 1,500 miles away in Washington DC. President Clinton was putting his signature on the Religious Freedom Restoration Act, an event which probably went unnoticed in Boerne.

In early December 1993, Greg Davis hand-carried the drawings to the Boerne City Hall on East Blanco Road, and as Davis recalls, "Everybody said, 'Hey, good to see you, we're ready to go with the project."[4] It should be noted that none of these informal words of encouragement and approval came from any of the town's elected officials or appointed members of the zoning board. The building inspector, a town employee to whom the plans had been presented, was required by law to either approve, reject, or propose changes within thirty days. If that period elapsed without any action by the building inspector, the plans were automatically approved. When the thirty-day period expired with no word from the building inspector, Davis called and told him that he was going to go ahead and put the job out for bids. According to his account, the inspector told him that he would get back to him. After not hearing anything for week, Davis called again and was told, "Oh, yeah, we're going to write you a letter."[5]

When the letter arrived, Davis learned to his dismay that the church was within the town's historic district and that it was the determination of the city council that the plans for the renovation of St. Peter's must be sent to the Historic Landmark Commission for their approval. Davis immediately called Father Tony Cummins at the church to inform him that the plans that seemed to be on the verge of approval had met a snag. Father Tony's surprised reaction was, "Oh gosh!"[6]

Since the Historic Landmark Commission declared that the church fell within the town's historic district despite the fact that it is fairly remote from the downtown area, the Planning and Zoning Commission proceeded to deny the demolition and building permit. The church lodged an appeal with the city council, and a meeting to hear the appeal was set for April 12, 1994. Mayor Heath recalled:

> It was a very lengthy meeting and I was very careful, as I am on any subject with any degree of significance, to allow a person to speak for the demolition and a person to speak against it. Back and forth. After lengthy discussion . . . the Council took a vote and denied the permit.[7]

At that point, the backers of the new church went to the Archdiocese (of San Antonio and Archbishop Flores) and charged that what the council had done in turning down the building permit was against the rules, and they encouraged the Archbishop to file a lawsuit. It was at this point that Father Tony, Greg Davis, and the proponents of the remodeled church heard from their attorney, Tom Drought, that they might have a remedy under the newly enacted Religious Freedom Restoration Act.[8]

RFRA Goes to Court

The law offered Father Tony and his allies a ready solution. "It seemed a pretty strong law in our favor," he recalled. "It seemed like a cakewalk. There were also private property issues under Texas law. It was our property to use as we wished, and if we were denied that use, then give us some compensation."[9] The backers of the church, however, decided not to simply sue under Texas or federal law for taking church property without just compensation, but rather to go to federal court and file suit under the Religious Freedom Restoration Act.[10]

It is not entirely clear how the final decision to resort to RFRA was made. Marci Hamilton, who was to represent the City of Boerne when the case eventually got to the US Supreme Court, believes one of the drafters of the RFRA legislation, University of Texas professor of law Douglas Laycock, had significant influence:

> Doug and Mark Stern [lawyer for the American Jewish Congress] were looking around the country for the right case [a test case to secure RFRA with an affirmation by the Supreme Court], and here was a case right in Doug's backyard. They also wanted a land use case because they thought that a land use case would never survive the compelling state interest test. They thought that the Court doesn't like historic preservation and this would be the perfect set of facts for their side.[11]

Laycock himself modestly downplayed his role in the drafting of RFRA, saying, "I had some hand in the drafting, although reports of my hand have been greatly exaggerated over the years."[12] He added that he had been working in the area of free exercise of religion cases for years and had gotten involved in the Oregon peyote case by drafting a major part of an *amicus curiae* brief on behalf of Smith and Black by fifty-five constitutional law scholars. Laycock identified his point of entry into the case as a call he received from Tom Drought, the attorney for the Archdiocese of San Antonio. "Tom," Laycock remembered, "was a good lawyer, but hadn't done any constitutional appeals before. He also called Mark Chopko, the lawyer for the Catholic Bishops Conference, and asked for some names, and Mark gave him some and he came up and took me to lunch and interviewed me. That's how I got into the case."[13]

Mayor Heath recalls the events of May 24, 1994:

> I was in my office which at that time was downstairs in City Hall and I was served papers by one of the deputy sheriffs or marshals, saying that it was the Archdiocese, as owner of the church property, alleging that we had violated the rights of the church, the

archdiocese, and the federal constitution, the state constitution, and the Religious Freedom Restoration Act of 1992.[14]

When asked whether he had been aware of the existence of RFRA at the time, Mayor Heath smiled and said, "No, but I became aware of it pretty quickly."[15]

The case was assigned to Federal District Court Judge Lucius Bunton, whose court sat in the town of Midland, and on August 5, 1994, he asked the parties to the suit whether they would agree to resolve the dispute through mediation. The mediation was held on October 28 in San Antonio and was presided over by a retired judge from Houston who was brought in to oversee the proceedings. Mayor Heath recalled, "The two sides never sat together. Our team would be in one room and the judge would come talk to us a while and then he'd go into another room and talk to the other team and bring stuff back and forth."[16]

It is at this point that the stories of mayor and the church architect diverge dramatically. Mayor Heath's version:

> At the end of the day, having looked at the model of what they had proposed and having been authorized by the council to make a decision and to propose something, I said that the council would consider the possibility of demolition if [the church] did two things: if they would save 80 percent of the historic structure from 1923 and lower slightly the apex of the roofline so that it doesn't overwhelm the structure . . . the other side said no.[17]

Architect Greg Davis has a different recollection:

> [The judge] asked us to mediate. We tried to mediate, and we came back. Actually, we had what we later ended up building. We gave that to the city but they turned us down. The city kept turning everything down. They would not accept us touching the building. There was no mediation on that.[18]

With a trial set in District Court, Judge Bunton convened a pretrial hearing in March 1995. The church was represented by Tom Drought, who had proposed suing under RFRA. The City of Boerne was represented by Lowell Denton. Until this point, the City of Boerne had not questioned the constitutionality of RFRA, but at the pretrial hearing, constitutionality was raised by Denton, who had been told about a law review article by Marci Hamilton, a professor at the Benjamin N. Cardozo School of Law of Yeshiva University in New York City, with the provocative title, "The Religious Freedom Restoration Act: Letting the Fox into the Henhouse Under Cover of Section Five of the Fourteenth Amendment."[19] The article, which argued that RFRA was unconstitutional, had yet to be published. Denton phoned Hamilton and asked if she could fax him the page proofs of the article, because Judge Bunton would be handing down his ruling at 5 PM that day. Hamilton recalls, "I got it over to him, I think, around two o'clock and Bunton ruled at five."[20]

The attorney for the church protested that it was too late to raise constitutional objections to RFRA, but Bunton dismissed these objections and, persuaded by Hamilton's argument, ruled on the spot that RFRA was unconstitutional because it exceeded the scope of Congress's enforcement powers under Section 5 of the Fourteenth Amendment. He referred the case on an expedited basis to the US Court of Appeals for the Fifth Circuit, which is located in New Orleans. For her last-minute assistance, which proved to be decisive, Marci Hamilton was rewarded by the city of Boerne. "They sent me some flowers," she said. "It was very nice."[21]

On January 23, 1996, the US Court of Appeals for the Fifth Circuit handed down a twenty-nine-page decision reversing Judge Bunton's ruling that RFRA was unconstitutional. Sitting in the courtroom in New Orleans as Douglas Laycock was arguing on behalf of the church, Mayor Heath recalls being stung by some of Laycock's arguments:

> I heard him say, among other things, words to this effect, "Well, Justices, what other way is the city of Boerne now going to find to strip the rights of citizens. . . ." We were not oppressive of the church. We were simply saying that every person, every family, every institution in our community must abide by the same rules—rules that were passed by duly elected officials of this city.[22]

For Heath and other opponents of the modification of the church, the question immediately before them was whether or not they would appeal the decision of the Fifth Circuit. There was only one avenue left to them—the US Supreme Court. A decision to appeal a case to Supreme Court is not taken lightly. Legal costs are enormous. and the odds that the Court will grant a writ of *certiorari* do not favor the appellant, especially if the parties of the other side oppose granting the writ.

Mayor Heath describes the events leading up to the decision:

> Things came to a head in October of 1996. I was finishing a bond-rating trip to New York and because of the delay out of LaGuardia [airport] and atrocious service by Northwest Airlines, I didn't get out of New York until 10 o'clock in the evening and the city council did all their business and then adjourned and waited for me to get there. Marci Hamilton was there, and after a lengthy discussion we made the decision on the basis of her recommendation and her own deliberations to appeal to the United States Supreme Court. She had told us that only 5 percent or so of appeals that are sent to the Court are heard, but that this issue was ripe. We eventually spent $325,000 through the whole process. The printing bill was over $10,000 alone."[23]

The town was spared the expense of the legal battle to get the Court to grant *certiorari* when the legal team representing the church and the archdiocese decided not to oppose it. They too wanted the issue decided by the Supreme Court. It was by no means certain that the Court would take the case. In all cases that had come before US courts of appeals testing the constitutionality of RFRA, the law had been found constitutional. The Supreme Court is more inclined to hear a case when there has been conflict among appeals courts as to the constitutionality of a piece of legislation. Recall, for example, that in the *Goldman* case involving the wearing of a yarmulke by an Air Force Officer, the Appeals Court of the District of Columbia took the case on appeal because several district courts were at odds over the constitutionality of the Air Force's ban on religious headgear.

The City of Boerne v. Flores, as the case was now designated, did offer several features that gave it a natural appeal for the justices. It was a First Amendment case, and, in the words of Boerne's lawyer, Marci Hamilton, "That's the kind of case that gets their attention."[24] There was one additional element of the case that made it constitutionally compelling: The Clinton administration had ordered the Department of Justice to intervene in the case on the side of the Archdiocese. A suit to which the United States government is a party marks it as a matter of considerable importance. Mayor Heath was not necessarily displeased by this development. "From that point on the lawsuit read, 'The City of Boerne Texas versus the Archdiocese of San Antonio and the United States of America,' so everybody was against us." For Mayor Heath, the case had a David and Goliath angle that he found appealing.[25]

Father Tony Cummins was optimistic that the Court would come out on his side. "I actually had a pretty good feeling because it had already been tried several times. I think our journey to the Supreme Court had four of five appeals courts rulings behind us in our favor."[26]

On October 15, 1996, the Supreme Court announced that it would hear *Boerne v. Flores*. The hearing was set for February 19, 1997; the city was to be represented by Marci Hamilton and the archdiocese by Douglas Laycock and the solicitor general of the United States, Walter Dellinger.[27] This was Hamilton's first oral argument before the Supreme Court, but she was well grounded in Court procedure, having clerked for Justice Sandra Day O'Connor.

Douglas Laycock's previous experience before the Court came in a case that reached the justices between *Smith v. Employment Division* and *Boerne v. Flores*. It was decided on June 11, 1993, about six months before the passage of RFRA. The full name of the case was *Church of the Lukumi Babalu Aye, Inc. v. The City of Hialeah* and was typical of most free exercise cases in that it involved a minor sect, a *Santería* church in Florida that practiced as one of its sacraments the sacrifice of animals. The city council of Hialeah enacted an ordinance making it a crime to inflict cruelty on animals. Although on the face of it the law appeared to apply broadly, it became clear to the justices that the council had targeted the Church of the Babalu Aye.

The Supreme Court, in a unanimous decision, found that the city ordinance violated the church's First Amendment right to free exercise of religion. It appeared for a moment that the Religious Freedom Restoration Act might be superfluous, but it was quickly observed that six of the nine justices who voted to overturn the city ordinance also used the occasion to reaffirm the opinion in the *Smith* case, saying that the Oregon law was one of general applicability, but that the Hialeah city council had singled out the church. Justices Souter, Blackmun, and O'Connor did not concur in Justice Kennedy's majority opinion, but used the occasion to criticize the Court's abandonment in the *Smith* case of the compelling state interest test.[28]

Reflecting on his feelings about his chances of success before the Supreme Court, Douglas Laycock recalled thinking that *Boerne* might just be the ideal case to take before the Supreme Court. Since the enactment of RFRA, a large number of suits had been filed by prison inmates claiming special religious privileges that were widely seen as frivolous and thus would have been more likely to result in the Court overturning RFRA. Corrections officials were complaining about the upsurge in religious movements that were filing suit under RFRA for such things as the right of American Indian prisoners to have access to a sweat lodge[29] to a group of Rastafarian corrections officers in New York State who challenged the Corrections Department's ban on dreadlocks for prison guards.[30] As Laycock recalls, an attorney from a religious organization supporting RFRA urged him not to oppose the granting of *certiorari* in *Boerne*:

> In two years, we might have a Rastafarian prisoner and a no-name lawyer, and we could have had Doug Laycock and the Archbishop of San Antonio. The [federal] government was in it on our side. The United States was defending the constitutionality of RFRA.[31]

RFRA Is Put to the Test

Boerne v. Flores began with the battle of the briefs. Six *amicus curiae* briefs were filed on behalf of the city of Boerne, mainly by historic preservation groups and state attorneys general on behalf of their prison systems, which had been deluged with RFRA claims. On the other side, twice as many were filed by religious liberty groups, churches, and members of Congress of both parties.

Making the case for the city, Marci Hamilton got strong hints that the justices were hostile to RFRA. "When we left the courtroom, I thought we would get nine votes. There was not a single justice who defended the law. . . . During oral arguments, not one of them thought it was a good law or defended the law."[32] Douglas Laycock was much less certain. "We spend much of our career in my field studying those nine people and trying to figure out what they do, but it doesn't mean that we can predict anything."[33]

Still, others seemed confident of victory for the church and RFRA. Hamilton recalls that members of the editorial board of the journal *Law and Religion* had a betting pool going on a listserv, "and the betting was something like twenty-seven to one that I would lose 9–0 and one guy was on the fence." As it turned out, neither side predicted exactly what the Court would do. Marci Hamilton's prediction of a 9–0 decision in her favor and the betting pool's 9–0 forecast that RFRA would be upheld were both wrong, but Hamilton's was closer to the mark. The Court by a 6–3 vote declared that Religious Freedom Restoration Act was unconstitutional.

Marbury Revisited

In the opinion written on behalf of the Court majority, consisting of himself and Justices Rehnquist, Stevens, Scalia, Thomas, and Ginsburg, Justice Anthony Kennedy laid out the objections to RFRA. After reviewing the act and quoting extensively from its preamble, Kennedy went right to the underlying constitutional justification for RFRA—that it represented a legitimate exercise of Congress's powers under Article 5 of the Fourteenth Amendment to enforce the guarantee in the amendment that no state shall deprive any person of "life, liberty, or property without due process of law," nor deny any person "equal protection of the laws." He then observed that the Church and the archbishop, backed by the United States government, made the case that RFRA represented permissible enforcement legislation. He then conceded that the Court had recognized Article 5 to be a positive grant of legislative power and cited a number of cases in which Congress legitimately used the enforcement power of Article 5.[34]

At this point in the opinion, Kennedy dropped his bomb:

Congress' power under Section 5 extends only to "enforc[ing]" the provisions of the Fourteenth Amendment. The Court has described this power as "remedial". . . . The design of the [Fourteenth] Amendment and the text of section 5 are inconsistent with the suggestion that Congress has the power to decree the substance of the Fourteenth Amendment's restrictions on the States. Legislation which alters the meaning of the Free Exercise Clause cannot be said to be enforcing the Free Exercise Clause. *Congress does not enforce a constitutional right by changing what the right is* [emphasis added].[35]

Rejecting the argument put forth by the attorneys for the church that since Congress has the power to protect citizens from racial discrimination under the Free Exercise clause of the Fourteenth Amendment, as it did with the Voting Rights Act of 1965, it should also have the power to use the same clause to promote religious liberty, Justice Kennedy asserted that there has been no pattern of deliberate religious discrimination in this country equivalent to the barriers erected against African Americans exercising their right to vote. This made RFRA, in his view, not a remedy but a congressional reaction so far out of proportion to the harm alleged by the church and its allies that it represented an effort by senators and House members to redefine portions of the Constitution.[36]

While the opinion condemned RFRA as an unlawful intrusion into areas reserved to the states, such as zoning, the most pointed comments were directed at Congress for attempting to impose its own interpretation of the Constitution. Justice O'Connor wrote:

> Our national experience teaches us that the Constitution is preserved best when each part of the government respects both the Constitution and the proper actions and determinations of the other branches. When the Court has interpreted the Constitution, it has acted within the province of the Judicial Branch. And while Congress's responsibilities to determine what laws are needed to safeguard the guarantees of the Fourteenth Amendment should be respected, Congress's discretion is not unlimited . . . and the courts retain the power, as they have since *Marbury v. Madison*, to determine if Congress has exceeded its authority under the Constitution.[37]

What was *Boerne v. Flores* all about? From one angle, it was a case involving federalism and the intrusion by Congress into an area reserved to the states. But it was even more a case about the separation of powers and the dispute between the Congress and the Supreme Court over who could legitimately determine the meaning of portions of the Constitution. All three branches of the federal government are necessarily jealous of the powers they enjoy under the Constitution. It is in the nature of the system of checks and balances that it should be so, and the battle over RFRA is a particularly intense and telling example of this power struggle between the branches.

Douglas Laycock, recalling why the Court's questioning of him and Solicitor General Walter Dellinger was so hostile, pointed out one feature of RFRA that seemed to antagonize the justices. "It had that terrible preamble. It was sort of in-your-face to the Court. I didn't realize how bad it was when the bill was going through."[38] The offensive passage in the bill's preamble was the statement that "in *Employment Division v. Smith* . . . the Supreme Court virtually eliminated the requirement that the government justify burdens on religious exercise imposed by laws neutral to religion."[39] Such a statement might not seem to us to be overly harsh, but Supreme Court justices do not like to be chided for being insufficiently protective of basic rights, especially by a co-equal branch of government. While stressing the importance of federalism as a factor in the outcome of the case, Laycock asserted that "*Boerne* really reduces Section 5 of the Fourteenth Amendment to an appendage of Section 1 [judicial enforcement of the amendment]. It takes out the independent means of enforcement for Congress. I think that's a big, big change."[40]

In this judgment, Laycock more or less agrees with his adversary, Marci Hamilton, who says that, "RFRA was an overreaching by Congress into the judicial role. I think the separation of powers question is as serious as the federalism problem." Using virtually the same language as Laycock, Hamilton recalled the hostile grilling given to her opponents and said, "They had to defend a law that was really in the Supreme Court's face so very directly, and the judges just did not have much time for that."[41]

Turf wars often descend to pettiness, even when issues of high constitutional importance are involved, and one could easily predict after the decision in *Boerne* that there would be another round in the volleying between Congress and the US Supreme Court. Having returned Congress's serve, the justices could expect Congress to send the ball back again with a nasty top spin.

Notes

1. Interview with Gregory Davis, San Antonio, Texas, March 30, 2003.
2. Interview with Mayor Patrick Heath, Boerne, Texas, March 28, 2003.
3. Interview with Gregory Davis.
4. Ibid.
5. Ibid. The fact that the thirty-day period had expired was used later in the Federal District Court to argue that the permit should have been granted without any further action. That argument was dismissed by the presiding judge, Lucius Bunton.
6. Ibid.
7. Patrick Heath interview.
8. Gregory Davis interview.
9. Interview with Father Tony Cummins, March 28, 2003.
10. Ibid.
11. Telephone interview with Marci Hamilton, March 21, 2003.
12. Telephone interview with Douglas Laycock, September 11, 2003.

13. Douglas Laycock interview.
14. Patrick Heath interview.
15. Ibid.
16. Ibid.
17. Ibid.
18. Gregory Davis interview.
19. 16 *Cardozo Law Review*, 357 (1994).
20. Marci Hamilton interview.
21. Ibid.
22. Patrick Heath interview.
23. Ibid.
24. Marci Hamilton interview.
25. Patrick Heath interview.
26. Father Tony Cummins interview.
27. The post of Solicitor General of the United States was created by Congress in 1870. He has been described as "the chief courtroom lawyer for the executive branch." Originally designed to assist the Attorney General, the Solicitor General has feet in both the legislative and judicial branches. The justices of the Supreme Court typically depend on the Solicitor General for recommendations on which cases to review. This function causes people to refer to him as "the tenth justice." Kermit L. Hall, ed. *The Oxford Companion to the Supreme Court of the United States* (New York: Oxford University Press, 1992), 802–803.
28. Cornell Clayton, "Law, Politics, and the Rehnquist Court: Structural Influences on Supreme Court Decision Making," in Howard Gillman and Cornell Clayton, eds., *The Supreme Court in American Politics* (Lawrence, KS: University of Kansas Press, 1999), 168–169.
29. *Hamilton v. Schriro*, 74 F.3d 1545 (8th Cir., January 12, 1996.)
30. *Francis v. Keane*, 888 F. Supp. 568 (S.D.N.Y. June 13, 1995.)
31. Douglas Laycock interview.
32. Marci Hamilton interview.
33. Douglas Laycock interview.
34. *Boerne v. Flores*, 521 US 507 (1997).
35. Ibid.
36. Ibid.
37. Ibid.
38. Douglas Laycock interview.
39. US Congress, Senate, 102nd Congress, 2nd Session, S. 2969, The Religious Freedom Restoration Act of 1992.
40. Douglas Laycock interview.
41. Marci Hamilton interview.

7

Congress Copes with *Boerne*

It took less than a month for Congress to convene a set of hearings and to receive the responses from the religious groups seeking to counteract the decision in the *Boerne* case. On July 14, 1997, the Subcommittee on the Constitution of the House Judiciary Committee was called to order by the chairman of the subcommittee, Rep. Charles T. Canady, a Florida Republican who represented Polk County, south of Orlando. Canady had made a name for himself since his election to the House in 1992.

A one-time Democrat, Canady had switched parties before he came to Congress and had become identified with issues of importance to social conservatives. In 1995 he sponsored a bill to forbid race or gender preferences in federal government hiring, and the following year was the House floor manager for the Defense of Marriage Act, which gives a state the right to refuse to recognize same-sex marriages performed in another state.[1]

The composition of the subcommittee chaired by Canady had a decidedly southern cast. Of its thirteen members, eight came from south of the Mason-Dixon line, where the fires of faith burn with great intensity. Among Republicans, with the exception of Rep. Henry Hyde, the chairman of the full Judiciary Committee and a member of the subcommittee, who was from Illinois, all members were southerners.

It has long been noted that regional biases are common on a number of congressional committees. The House Interior Committee was loaded with representatives from the far West and Mountain states. Even on the House Appropriations Committee, whose chairmen strove for more balance in their membership, Midwesterners were overrepresented and Easterners underrepresented.[2]

The strong representation of Southern Republicans on the subcommittee made it an appealing target for representatives of religious groups, who knew that they would find a hospitable environment to make their case for undoing the effects of *Boerne*.

It would be a mistake, however, to conclude that the subcommittee's Democrats were indifferent or hostile to the pleas of religious groups. Rep. Jerrold Nadler had inherited many Orthodox Jewish constituents from Rep. Steven Solarz's old district, and Reps. Robert C. Scott of Virginia, John Conyers, Jr., of Michigan, and Melvin L. Watt of North Carolina represented districts with particularly influential African American churches. Perhaps the most conspicuous indication that this set of hearings would favor the opponents of the Supreme Court decision was the title of the hearings: Protecting Religious Freedom After *Boerne v. Flores*.

In a manner typical of all congressional hearings, the proceedings began with an opening statement by the chairman, Rep. Canady, who set the stage for the event by asserting that the most important issue to be discussed would be "the Court's holding regarding the role of the Congress in interpreting the Constitution and protecting individual liberties [which] raised troubling issues concerning the relationship between the judiciary and the elected representatives of the people in the Legislative branch."[3]

The tone of testimony by six of the seven witnesses who testified was defiant and the predictions apocalyptic. More than one witness likened the *Boerne* decision to that in the Dred Scott case in 1857 denying blacks the right to citizenship. Perhaps the most measured testimony came from Marc Stern, director of the Legal Department of the American Jewish Congress, who counseled against trying to reverse *Boerne* by attempting to ratify a constitutional amendment, which, he warned, might precipitate a constitutional crisis. He urged that "Congress ought not sort of throw it in the face of the Supreme Court, nor," he added, "ought it go quietly into the night."[4]

The only voice supporting the Supreme Court's decision came late in the hearings from Jeff Sutton, the Solicitor of the state of Ohio. Sutton, whose state had filed an *amicus curiae* brief against RFRA when the *Boerne* case went to the Supreme Court, argued that RFRA had spawned a flood of lawsuits by prison inmates and pointed out that 60 percent of all cases filed under RFRA were from prisoners claiming that their religions demanded everything from animal sacrifice to the distribution of racist literature and that corrections officials had banned them from these practices. The lawsuits filed by prisoners were diverting wardens and other prison officials from their jobs. Sutton's testimony was filled with horror stories such as the RFRA suit by members of the Luciferian cult in Wyoming to allow them to burn Christian hymnals and bibles as part of their religious ritual.[5] A written statement from the attorney general of Florida made many of the same points about frivolous prison lawsuits.

The Senate lagged behind the House in holding hearings in the aftermath of *Boerne*, but not by much. On October 1, 1997, Senate Judiciary Committee Chairman Orrin G. Hatch [R-UT] called the hearings to order in the Dirksen Senate Office Building. After noting that the beginning of the hearings auspiciously coincided with the eve of the Jewish high holy day Rosh Hashanah, Hatch read at length a quotation on religious freedom by James Madison, which, he quickly added, "stands in stark contrast to the recent pronouncements of the Supreme Court in such cases as *Employment Division v. Smith.*" In response to this, Hatch said, "Congress passed the Religious Freedom Restoration Act . . . with only three dissenting votes in the entire Congress. In the recent *City of Boerne* case, however, the Court decided that RFRA went beyond Congress's power under the Fourteenth Amendment as applied to the States."[6]

The purpose of the hearings was to explore ways that Congress could reconstruct RFRA, or at least something approximating it, without exceeding the constitutional powers of Congress. The leadoff witness was Professor Douglas Laycock of the University of Texas Law School, who had argued for the Archdiocese of San Antonio before the Supreme Court in the *Boerne* case. Laycock laid out for the committee the options, which had been significantly narrowed by the Supreme Court's determination that the use of Section 5 of the Fourteenth Amendment to reinstate the *Sherbert* rule was unconstitutional and by the Court's decision in another case quite unrelated to free exercise of religion questions.

Guns and God

The case was *United States v. Lopez*,[7] in which the Supreme Court held unconstitutional the Gun-Free Schools Act of 1990. The authority under which Congress passed this law, the purpose of which was to make it a federal crime to carry a gun within a certain zone around a school, was the Commerce Clause of Article I, Section 8, of the Constitution, which gives Congress the power "to regulate commerce . . . among the several states." The majority on the Court could not see how the carrying of a gun near a school had any adverse effect on interstate commerce that would necessitate regulation by Congress. The Supreme Court had upheld the Commerce Clause as the source of constitutional authority for the Civil Rights Act of 1964, which forbade discrimination in public accommodations,[8] but it is obviously easier to make a connection between the Commerce Clause and discriminatory practices in hotels located on interstate highways than between the Commerce Clause and guns in schoolyards.

It is important to note here that an act of Congress can be deemed unconstitutional for one or more of several reasons. The most obvious one, of course, would be legislation that abridged a fundamental right set forth in the Bill of Rights. Another might be an act of Congress that violated the doctrine of separation of powers. Yet another is Congress passing laws that transgress the rules of federalism by usurping powers reserved to the states in the Constitution.While the Commerce Clause has proven an important constitutional basis for congressional action, the *Lopez* case made clear that it cannot be stretched beyond a certain point.

So if Section 5 of the Fourteenth Amendment was closed off to Congress and the use of the Commerce Clause was now uncertain, were there other avenues that could be pursued? There was, of course, Congress's power of the purse, which might be used by Congress to bar religious discrimination in programs receiving federal money. Laycock also urged Congress to assert that the *Boerne* decision applied only to the states and that RFRA was still constitutional as applied to acts by the federal government. But, in the end, Laycock conceded that the Supreme Court would likely find the simple reenactment of RFRA by Congress unconstitutional.[9]

RLPA, the First Offspring of RFRA

The result of the hearings chaired by Rep. Canady in the aftermath of the *Boerne* decision was the Religious Liberty Protection Act of 1998, or RLPA. Canady's subcommittee reported the bill out favorably to the full House Judiciary Committee, but no further action was taken in 1998. The 105th Congress ended with the bill not even acted upon by the full Judiciary Committee. Nonetheless, a substantial record had been built up in the hearings in Canady's subcommittee.

When the 106th Congress convened in January 1999, the sponsors of the bill were ready to press ahead with it. Since it was not enacted in the previous Congress, it needed to be reintroduced in the new one. This took place on May 5, 1999, and the bill was now designated H.R. 1691 (House Bill 1691).

A new set of hearings began in Canady's subcommittee a week later, on May 12, 1999. A markup of the bill took place only two weeks after that. A markup is the first opportunity to amend a bill. Votes are taken in the committee or subcommittee to add, delete, or change language; each change must be voted on, and the votes of each committee member are recorded for or against the amendments. The bill, with the amendments added in markup, was reported out favorably to the full Judiciary Committee. Because of the record built up in the previous Congress, the bill was familiar to the members of the full committee and appeared to be on the fast track to enactment by the House.

Speed Bumps for RLPA

RLPA's sponsors had decided on a two-pronged approach to achieving in RLPA what they had failed to achieve in RFRA. For the land use portion of the bill (the area of the law involved in the *Boerne* case), the constitutional authority would come from the Commerce Clause, even though the Court had rejected this approach both in the gun-free schools case and in *Boerne*. The second section of the bill, dealing with the religious rights of inmates in state prisons, would find its constitutional authority in the Spending Clause of Article I. This section of the bill would forbid federally supported state prisons to abridge the free exercise of an inmate's religion without a compelling state interest.

Opposition to the approach taken by the Republican majority came from four Democrats, who disputed the constitutional justifications for RFRA offered by the Republicans, The Democrats, Rep. Jerrold Nadler of New York, Rep. Howard Berman of California, Rep. William Delahunt of Massachusetts, and Rep. Sheila Jackson Lee of Texas, questioned whether, in light of the Court's decision in the *Lopez* case (the Gun-Free Schools Act) the Commerce Clause would enable RLPA's sponsors to establish a connection between a local zoning dispute and interstate commerce. They also challenged the applicability of the Spending Clause as leverage against the states, requiring them to demonstrate a compelling state interest if they curtailed the free exercise rights of an inmate in a state prison that received federal funds.

The opponents further believed that if RLPA were passed, it would enable employers or landlords, based on their sincere religious beliefs, to deny jobs or housing to certain groups of people, overriding state and local antidiscrimination laws. The four House

Democrats supported an amendment offered by Rep. Nadler, who argued:

> . . . [T]he religious liberty defense could be asserted against federal civil rights plaintiffs in cases concerning disability, sexual orientation, familial status, and pregnancy. Employers in non-religiously-affiliated organizations, for example, may assert the religious liberty defense against gay or lesbian applicants.[10]

Both the subcommittee and the full Judiciary Committee rejected Nadler's amendment. On May 26, 1999, the subcommittee met and voted to report favorably to the full committee the bill H.R. 1691, the Religious Liberty Protection Act. On June 23, the full Judiciary Committee met and reported the bill out to the House by voice vote.

It might strike us as odd that members of the committee did not want to go on record supporting a bill as popular as RLPA. As we have seen, members like to take credit for supporting bills that are popular with voters, and a recorded vote documents that support. With a voice vote, the chairman calls for ayes and nays and determines, based on the volume of responses for each side, whether the bill passes or is voted down, and there is no printed record of how any members voted. RLPA was so non-controversial that many members did not even bother to attend the meeting. Had a recorded vote been taken, the absentees would have been in the embarrassing position of having to explain why they were not present to endorse so worthy a piece of legislation.

Where the Rules Rule

On July 15, 1999, RLPA came to the floor of the House. Under House procedures, each bill is usually preceded by a rule which governs the manner in which the bill will be debated. The rule must be approved before the bill itself can be taken up. Failure to adopt the rule kills the accompanying bill. The rule for RLPA passed easily.

A rule is obtained when a member of the committee that had jurisdiction over the bill, in this case the Judiciary Committee, goes before the House Rules Committee to request a rule to accompany the bill. Rules come in a variety of forms. A "closed rule" means that the bill cannot be amended. An "open rule" means that any member can offer an amendment. There are also "modified rules" that, for example, might allow amendments on one part of a bill but not on another or permit some named members to offer amendments but bar anyone else. The Rules Committee is assumed to have the approval of the majority party and the Speaker, who appoints the members of the Rules Committee. The Republicans wanted to prevent amendments to RLPA, so they introduced a closed rule.

The rule is generally introduced to the House by the chairman of the Rules Committee or a member of that committee who is in the majority party. In the case of RLPA, it was Rep. Sue Myrick of North Carolina, a conservative Republican in her third term in the House. Known as a forceful, even confrontational member, she was held in high regard by her party's leaders. Evidence of that confidence was her membership on the Rules Committee, where party leaders place only their most trusted colleagues.

After a brief debate, the rule was approved, but not before a perennial House gadfly, Rep. Ron Paul, a Texas Republican and the 1988 Libertarian presidential candidate, rose to say that although he favored the rule, he opposed RLPA itself. Rep. Paul was to set something of a record in the House between 1999 and 2002 by casting the only dissenting vote on fifty-one bills. He even opposed awarding the congressional gold medal to Charles Schulz, the creator of the "Peanuts" comic strip.[11]

Paul's objection to RLPA was characteristically unconventional. He argued that by restoring a standard—any standard, even that of compelling state interest—Congress was authorizing the abridgment of free exercise of religion. RLPA, he asserted, "authorizes government to substantially burden a person's free exercise if the government demonstrates some nondescript compelling interest to do so."[12]

After adoption of the rule, the House proceeded to deal with the substance of RLPA, beginning with a statement by Rep. Canady citing the benefits of RFRA before it was declared unconstitutional. Under RFRA, he pointed out, an organization that fed homeless people had filed suit after their soup kitchen had been held in violation of local zoning laws. He mentioned a lawsuit by a professor of religious law at The Catholic University of America who had been denied tenure and had sued under the statute, and a successful legal challenge by a prison inmate denied permission by guards to wear a crucifix.[13]

Supporters of the Nadler substitute resumed their argument that RLPA might be used to trump state antidiscrimination laws and would "enable the CEO of a large corporation to say, 'My religion prohibits me from letting my corporation hire a divorced person or a disabled person, or a mother who should be home with her children and not at work, or a gay or lesbian person' . . . and never mind that the states' civil rights laws prohibit that kind of discrimination."[14]

Later in the debate, Canady produced a letter from the Department of Justice that offered the opinion that RLPA, if enacted, would be upheld as constitutional. He was followed by another speaker who reeled off the names of twenty religious groups that supported the bill. The list ranged from the B'nai B'rith to the US Catholic Conference and from the Christian Coalition to the NAACP. Another message came from the White House. It promised that if Congress passed RLPA, President Clinton would sign it. Since members of Congress do not relish spending time on a bill that is destined to be vetoed, it was reassuring to know that the work of the members would not be in vain.

At the end of the debate, on July 15, 1999, Rep. Nadler and his Democratic colleagues offered their bill as a substitute. It was rejected by a vote of 234–190. All but a half-dozen of those supporting the Nadler amendment were Democrats. All but a handful of those rejecting it were Republicans. With the Nadler amendment disposed of, the House could then move on to final passage, and by a vote of 306 to 118, the Religious Liberty Protection Act moved one step closer to passage.

The Senate Takes Its Time

RLPA reached the Senate just at the time that it was scheduled to take its annual August recess. But the delay for RLPA would likely be more than a month because Congress, upon its return after Labor Day, needed to pass the annual appropriations bills that provide the money for the federal government to operate for the following year. These bills must be passed by September 30, and, except in unusual circumstances, the month of September is given over to them. The fall calendar of Congress, moreover, contains several week-long recesses for Veterans' Day, Thanksgiving, and the Christmas holidays. Accordingly, sponsors of the Senate's companion measure to the House's H.R. 1691 did not get around to introducing it until February 22, 2000, when S.2081, the Senate version, was introduced by Senator Orrin Hatch [R-UT], chairman of the Senate Judiciary Committee. Hatch's committee was given jurisdiction over the bill and hearings were planned.

At this point the differences between the House and the Senate emerged dramatically. In the House, we recall, the Nadler amendment was rejected first by a subcommittee of the Judiciary Committee, next by the full committee, and finally by the House as a whole. Its sponsor, Rep. Nadler, was a Democrat, as were the bulk of his supporters. The amendment, accordingly, stood little chance of success in the face of opposition by the Republican majority. In the Senate, however, the same concerns about RLPA raised by Nadler were taken up by Senator Edward M. Kennedy [D-MA], one of the most senior members of the Senate Judiciary Committee. Unlike the House, where the views of the minority are easily turned aside, the minority in the Senate has impressive powers of obstruction and possesses the ultimate weapon to use against a bill they oppose—the filibuster.

Much of the routine business conducted in the Senate is by unanimous consent. In order to proceed with business, all senators must agree. Withholding consent and, in the extreme, using extended debate, or even the threat of it, to block consideration of a piece of business is a power enjoyed by all senators and gives each one of them great bargaining power.

While no filibuster was threatened against RLPA in the Senate, the objections to the House version of the bill by Senator Kennedy and others meant that S.2081 would be unlikely to pass unless his concerns were met. Kennedy's objections were essentially those that had been expressed by Rep. Nadler in the House, but other Democrats had objections of their own. Senator Harry Reid, the Assistant Democratic Minority Leader (or Whip), objected to the RLPA provisions that protected the free exercise rights of prisoners. Reid said, "It was my belief, one that I continue to hold, that prisoners in this country have become entirely too litigious. Frivolous lawsuits seem to be the norm, not the exception to the rule."[15]

Negotiations between Hatch and dissatisfied Democrats continued through the spring of 2000, and on July 13, 2000, just two weeks before the Senate's August recess, Hatch introduced a modified form of RLPA, designed to meet the objections of the Democrats. The bill was renumbered S.2869 and given a new but cumbersome title, the Religious Land Use and Institutionalized Persons Act of 2000.

RLUIPA: Does It Meet the Constitutional Test?

It always helps to have a catchy acronym for your legislation, preferably one that trips off the tongue. The cumbersomely titled Inter-modal Surface Transportation Efficiency Act was invariably referred to as "Ice Tea." The North American Free Trade Act (NAFTA) was followed by the Central American Free Trade Act (CAFTA); both are easily pronounced. But the successor to RLPA, the Religious Land Use and Institutionalized Persons Act, produced the clumsy acronym RLUIPA. The agreed-upon pronunciation was "ARLOOPA," which sounds suspiciously like a disease of the nerve endings. Nonetheless, it proved to be no less popular than its predecessor with members of Congress.

From the day it was introduced by Senator Hatch on July 13, 2000, until it was presented to President Clinton for his signature on September 22, barely two months elapsed. This modified version of RLPA required no new hearings at either the subcommittee or full committee level in either house of Congress. When on July 27, 2000, Hatch asked for unanimous consent to proceed with consideration of the bill, there was no objection.

After bestowing praise on his cosponsor, Senator Kennedy, and on Senators Strom Thurmond and Harry Reid, both of whom had objected to portions of RLUIPA but did not stand in the way of its passage, Hatch also commended chairman Canady of the House Constitution Subcommittee and expressed the hope that the House would speedily pass the bill with the changes that had been added by the Senate. The Senate then passed RLUIPA unanimously.

At 6:20 PM on the very day that the Senate had passed the bill, Rep. Canady was on the floor of the House asking for unanimous consent to take up the Senate bill. The Senate, by changing RLPA to meet Senator Kennedy's objections and retitling it, had made it into a different bill than the one that the House had originally passed. Accordingly, the House needed to agree to the changes made in the bill by the Senate or reject them and force the bill to go to a conference committee.

A conference was not needed for RLUIPA. The House merely accepted the Senate bill, because pressure was building from the various religious groups to get the bill to the President as quickly as possible for his signature.

Just a few formalities needed to be attended to before the House voted. One was for Rep. Canady to reciprocate Senator Hatch's praise. Another was a victory speech of sorts by Rep. Nadler who, thanks to the timely intervention of Senator Kennedy, had gotten most of what he had been denied in the House.

Nadler did not gloat but was clearly pleased:

> This is the third in a series of bills we have considered on the floor in the last seven years to deal with some Supreme Court decisions from the early nineties. It is extremely important for

the preservation of some of the free exercise protections of the Constitution, for the free exercise of religion. It is different, more narrow, than the Religious Liberty Protection Act we considered on the floor last year. That bill, you may recall, had some people concerned with some civil rights implications. Those concerns have been allayed.[16]

The House then approved RLUIPA by a voice vote. Rep. Canady returned to the floor of the House on Thursday, September 21, 2000, to declare, "Mr. Speaker, tomorrow, the President of the United States will sign into law The Religious Land Use and Institutionalized Persons Act, a bill I was proud to sponsor with . . . the gentleman from New York, Mr. Nadler. . . . This Act will protect the free exercise of religion from unnecessary government interference."[17]

But, as we have seen in earlier cases, issues that appear to have been settled have a tendency to rise from the grave like disembodied spirits. In this fashion, despite the apparently unanimous support the final version of the bill received in both houses, some members were unreconciled, and not all interest groups were pleased.

Shortly before President Clinton signed the bill, Senator Strom Thurmond issued the warning that, "There are legitimate issues regarding whether S.2869 is constitutional. Moreover, there are serious questions about whether this bill is good public policy, especially as it relates to the prisons and jails across America." He added, "The bill is entirely inconsistent with the principles of federalism."[18]

Thurmond's warning was echoed by a lobbyist for the National Association of Counties, who also raised the danger flag that RLUIPA violated the principle of federalism. "This bill," he said, "is squarely aimed at preempting local authority. From the local perspective, this bill is as bad as it ever was."[19]

Federalism and Free Exercise

The issue being raised by the lobbyist was whether Congress had exceeded its constitutional authority under the Commerce Clause to legislate in an area that was traditionally under the jurisdiction of the states. There is no function of government more clearly a matter for state and local government than zoning. We would be indignant if Congress, for example, involved itself in approving backyard swimming pools or the number of townhouses that can be built on a piece of land. Imagine House members and senators being distracted from the national economy, international terrorism, and global trade to deal with boundary disputes between homeowners or whether a convenience store can be located in a residential area. But when one party in a zoning dispute is a church, or any other institution that tends to attract Congress's sympathetic attention, the problem gets more complicated.

Congress, as we have seen, is responsive to the anxieties of religious groups who believe that the free exercise of religion is being curtailed by some act of government. As we have also seen, standing up for religion is one of the most popular acts for an elected official, who depends upon popular support for reelection. And while Congress is not generally reckless in its exercise of power, the impulse to do the popular or necessary thing may sometimes cause its members to be less than restrained about exercising their constitutional authority in enacting laws that are popular or, in its eyes, necessary.

Since the late 1930s, the Commerce Clause has been the authority under which Congress has legislated in fields as diverse as agriculture and civil rights. The Supreme Court had ruled unconstitutional a series of laws passed by Congress to further the economic recovery of the United States from the Great Depression. The basis of several of these rulings was that Congress had exceeded its authority under the Commerce Clause to regulate economic activities. Starting in the late 1930s, the justices began to view the use of the Commerce Clause more charitably, and in the case of *National Labor Relations Board v. Jones & Laughlin*, upheld a sweeping application of the Commerce Clause. Chief Justice Charles Evans Hughes wrote:

> Although activities may be *intra*state in character when separately considered, if they have such a close and substantial relation to

interstate commerce that their control is essential or appropriate to protect that commerce from burdens and obstructions, Congress cannot be denied the power to exercise that control.[20]

What followed was an almost uninterrupted period of forty years in which the Supreme Court approved of major exercises of congressional power using the Commerce Clause until 1995, when the Supreme Court handed down its decision in *US v. Lopez*, the gun-free schools case. Five years later, it struck down a portion of the Violence Against Women Act as an improper use of the Commerce Clause.[21]

If the Supreme Court looked so unfavorably on the use of the Commerce Clause to protect school children from guns and providing legal remedies for women who had been the victims of violence, what was the likelihood that the Court would smile on the use of the clause to help churches in zoning disputes? As of this writing, that part of RLUIPA has not yet been addressed by the Supreme Court, but land use was only one half of RLUIPA.

Protecting Prison Pieties

The other half of RLUIPA concerned the right of free exercise of religion for those in state prisons. Here, Congress sought its constitutional authority not only from the Commerce Clause, but also from the Spending Clause of Article I.

RLUIPA's requirement that state prison officials accommodate the religious requirements of inmates unless there is a compelling state interest not to was challenged by prison authorities in Ohio. They claimed that Section 3 of RLUIPA was unconstitutional because it elevated religion to an improper degree, thus violating the Establishment Clause of the Constitution, the clause that comes before the Free Exercise clause. The Supreme Court held that RLUIPA did not violate the establishment clause,[22] and since Ohio authorities did not raise the question of whether RLUIPA violated the Commerce and Spending clauses, the Court did not address them and based its decision solely on the Establishment Clause. The State of Ohio could still challenge the constitutionality of the law on those two provisions of the Bill of Rights. The land use question was not addressed at all.

The Ohio case, *Cutter v. Wilkinson*, while only a partial vindication of RLUIPA, makes an important point at a time when judges are being assailed for being hostile to religion. Certainly, decisions such as those in *Smith* and *Boerne* could lead some people to that conclusion. But since it involved a group of convicts, some of them adherents to a very unconventional white supremacist religious sect, the Ohio decision looks very much like the Court bending over backward to protect free exercise of religion.

Justices of the Supreme Court and members of Congress probably do not differ much on the role of religion in American life. They form a reasonably heterogeneous assemblage from a variety of religious backgrounds; there is not a militant atheist among the group. It is the Constitution, the meaning of the Free Exercise Clause, and the manner in which each institution views the separation of powers, that demarcate the differences. The elements that go into forming that line of demarcation is the subject of the next chapter.

Notes

1. Michael Barone and Grant Ujifusa, *The Almanac of American Politics, 1998* (Washington DC: National Journal, 1997), 371–372.
2. Richard F. Fenno, Jr., *Congressmen in Committees* (Boston: Little, Brown, 1973), passim, and *The Power of the Purse* (Boston: Little, Brown, 1966), 59–60.
3. U.S. Congress. House Committee on the Judiciary, Hearing before the Subcommittee on the Constitution, *Protecting Religious Freedom After Boerne v. Flores*. 105th Congress, 1st sess., July 14, 1997, 2.
4. *Protecting Religious Freedom*, 16.
5. *Protecting Religious Freedom*, 59–61.
6. US Congress. Senate. Committee on the Judiciary, Hearing before the Judiciary Committee of the United States Senate on *Congress' Constitutional Role in Protecting Religious Liberty*. 105th Congress, 2nd sess. October 1, 1997, 2.
7. 514 US 549 (1995).
8. *Heart of Atlanta Motel v. United States*, 379 US 241 (1964).

9. US Senate, Congress' Constitutional Role in Protecting Religious Liberty, 9.

10. US Congress, House of Representatives, Committee on the Judiciary, *Religious Liberty Protection Act of 1999, Report Together with Dissenting and Additional Views.* Report 106–219, 106th Congress, 1st sess., 1999, 38.

11. David Hawkings and Brian Nutting, eds., *CQ's Politics in America, 2004* (Washington DC: CQ Press, 2003), 979.

12. US Congress, House, *Religious Liberty Protection Act of 1999, Congressional Record*, H5581.

13. *Religious Liberty Protection Act of 1999*, H5588.

14. *Religious Liberty Protection Act of 1999*, H5589.

15. US Congress, Senate, *Congressional Record*, July 27, 2000, S7778–S7779.

16. US Congress, House, *Congressional Record*, July 27, 2000, H7191–H7192.

17. US Congress, House, *Congressional Record*, September 21, 2000, H1563.

18. US Congress, Senate, *Congressional Record*, September 22, 2000, S7991.

19. Matthew Tully, "Religious Liberties Compromise Bill Ready to Go in Senate," *CQ Monitor News*, July 25, 2000.

20. *N.L.R.B. v. Jones & Laughlin Steel Corp.*, 301 U.S. 49 (1937).

21. *US v. Morrison*, 529 U.S. 598 (2000).

22. *Cutter et al. v. Wilkinson, Director, Ohio Department of Rehabilitation and Correction, et al.* No. 03-9877. Decided May 31, 2005.

8

Strangers on a Hill

The Supreme Court building is just a block away from the three Senate office buildings on Capitol Hill, but in many ways, it might just as well be on the other side of the world. Originally located in the Capitol itself, the Supreme Court moved to its own building in 1935 and now stands in lofty alabaster isolation on First Street, NE. The old Supreme Court chamber, located in the Capitol, is a favorite stop for tourists, but is no more than a relic of a time when two of the three branches of the federal government lived under one roof.

The physical separation of the Court from Congress finds its parallel in another kind of separation—an array of differences, some only minor tensions and other serious conflicts, between these two institutions. Some of these frictions arise quite naturally from the very nature of the separation of powers. Still others emerge from the different characteristics of these two institutions, such as varying interpretations of principles central to the Constitution. We saw both kinds of friction in the Supreme Court's refusal to grant powers of interpretation claimed by Congress under Section 5 of the Fourteenth Amendment in the case of *Boerne v. Flores.*

Differing views on the question of free exercise of religion have proven a particularly raw point of friction between the Court and Congress over the last two decades. The reason for this is clear—no area of American life is more sensitive than religion.

Churches feel threatened by the zoning decisions of cities whose officials sometimes prefer that land be used by homes or businesses, which generate property tax revenue and economic activity, rather than churches, which are usually tax-exempt. Likewise, wardens of prisons concerned about maintaining order in a violent and unruly place look differently at the desire of Native American inmates to practice their religion by establishing a sweat lodge in the prison yard than do the prisoners.

The rawness and sensitivity of the free exercise question, then, feeds into clear institutional differences between the branches of the federal government, especially between Congress and the nonelected judges with their lifetime tenure. These tensions and conflicts can descend to nasty turf battles that we would consider unseemly if they were not waged by people in black robes and business suits.

Institutional Friction

To begin at the most basic level, the federal court system depends for its livelihood on money appropriated by Congress. Congress can also add to the courts' case load by declaring a problem to be of such transcendent importance that only a federal solution is adequate. We saw this when Congress gave abused women the right under the Violence against Women Act to sue their attackers in federal court, but the Supreme Court could find no connection between acts of violence against women and interstate commerce.

Some stresses stem perhaps from irritations of a purely personal nature. In recent years, justices of the Supreme Court have emerged badly battered from the polarized, partisan, and contentious confirmation process in the Senate, so it would not be surprising if they were to harbor lingering bitterness towards the politicians who subjected them to harsh and lengthy interrogation. Few Supreme Court justices would ever admit to feelings of resentment, although Clarence Thomas did characterize his 1991 confirmation hearing as a "high-tech lynching." Still, a recently confirmed member of the high court must feel as if he or she had just escaped the clutches of the Spanish Inquisition. While we imagine that justices are men and women of godlike composure and steady temperament, it is certainly possible that some might feel abused by the confirmation process and what it demands of them.

On the other side of Constitution Avenue, senators experience the most acute frustration as they struggle to extract the views of nominees to the Supreme Court who have been well briefed by the Justice Department on how to steer clear of statements that would doom their chances of being confirmed. No slouches as interrogators, the senators on the Judiciary Committee must sometimes feel blinded by a cloud of conversational smoke laid down by nominees who have been warned by their Justice Department briefers that excessive candor could lead to disaster.

Over the years, the Senate has rejected several Supreme Court nominees. Twenty-six nominees have been rejected or withdrew their names from consideration—one in six of the names sent up to Capitol Hill. Senator Strom Thurmond of South Carolina, who was instrumental in blocking Associate Justice Abe Fortas from being elevated to Chief Justice, set the tone for these probing inquiries into the thinking of judicial nominees. In 1968 he said, "The Supreme Court has assumed such a powerful role as a policymaker in the Government that the Senate must necessarily be concerned with the views of the prospective Chief Justices."[1]

Presidents, frustrated with the Senate's opposition to their nominees, sometimes resort to unusual tactics to seat a nominee. In 2004 President Bush used his prerogative to make recess appointments of Appeals Court nominees whose confirmations had been blocked by Democrats. These appointments expire with the end of the session in which they are made, but some recess appointees have ultimately been confirmed.

Presidents are sometimes tempted to nominate a senator to the Supreme Court. The reasoning here is that the Senate would be disinclined to turn down one of its own. Between 1888 and 1937, the Senate did not even require Judiciary Committee hearings for senators nominated to the Supreme Court. In 1937, hearings on Justice Hugo L. Black, a former senator, took place after he was confirmed, only when it came to light that he had been a member of the Ku Klux Klan.

When Associate Justice Fortas stepped down from the Court, President Lyndon B. Johnson decided to send to the Senate the name of Senator Philip Hart, a well-liked Michigan Democrat. Hart politely declined the offer, saying he was "comfortable in the Senate."[2] Given the polarization in the Senate today—for example, the massive opposition to the confirmation of ex-Senator John Ashcroft for Attorney General in 2001 and the outright rejection of ex-Senator John Tower for Secretary of Defense a decade earlier—looking to the Senate for nominees to fill Supreme Court vacancies no longer offers a sure path to success for presidents.

Once a justice is seated on the Court, any residual feelings of having been abused by the confirmation process are soon augmented by other sources of tension with Congress that are more institutional than personal, although the personal feelings may never entirely disappear. The sources of institutional tension will occupy us for the remainder of this chapter and shape the conclusions of this book.

Congress's Disappearing Judges

It has been estimated that in the early years of this country about 15 percent of all new members of Congress had some judicial experience in their backgrounds. This percentage persisted for the next several decades, when the percentage stabilized at 10 percent. In the twentieth century, prior judicial service by members of Congress declined, so that by the 100th Congress (1989–91), only seven members of the House and five Senators had held judicial positions. The numbers are just as small when the legislative backgrounds of Supreme Court justices are examined. As of 1988, 106 individuals had served on the US Supreme Court. Of that number, only twelve had served in Congress—eight senators and four representatives. The last senator to serve was Justice Harold H. Burton, who was nominated by Harry Truman in

1945.[3] Among recent justices of the Supreme Court, only Justice Sandra Day O'Connor had legislative experience, having served in the Arizona Senate.

One obvious reason for the decline in legislators who gain judicial experience either before or after congressional service is the growth of careerism on Capitol Hill. In the nineteenth century, it was common for members of Congress to serve only a few terms, or even a single one, as Abraham Lincoln did, and then return to business, farming, or the law, and perhaps become a judge later. Today, members of Congress, once elected, use all of the advantages of their incumbency to prolong their service and acquire the benefits of seniority, such as committee chairmanships. This is even more marked in the House than in the Senate because of the political gerrymandering of House districts to benefit incumbents.[4]

Lawyers are still the most prevalent professionals in Congress, and justices of the Supreme Court are also lawyers, but that forges no special bond between them. Presiding over a court is quite a bit different from pleading a case before one, and the decreasing lack of common experience may contribute to the psychological distance between those serving in Congress and those on the federal bench, but it is probably not a major factor.

Textual Deviation

Unlike the categorical clarity of the Ten Commandments, acts of Congress are not self-evident or self-explanatory. Even if those drafting the bills in Congress were masters of the most exquisite verbal precision, their work would still be subject to conflicting interpretations. Those given the task of carrying out the will of Congress—civil servants in the executive branch or in the many independent regulatory agencies such as the Federal Communications Commission or the Securities and Exchange Commission—are accorded considerable discretion in carrying out that will. They enjoy this discretion because there is simply no way that even the most carefully drawn statute could anticipate every particular situation that arises. And, as James Q. Wilson pointed out, Congress often has little interest in the supervision of these agencies once they have been created. "The courts," he wrote, "provide a ready and willing forum in which contending interests may struggle over the justification and interpretation of specific rules and practices."[5]

"Statutory interpretation" is the term that applies to courts attempting to figure out what Congress meant when it enacted a particular law. One device used to make this determination is the legislative history of a particular law. Such a history would include everything from the bill as it was originally introduced to the record of the hearings on the bill in both houses, the committee reports, the debates on the floor of both chambers, and even the "colloquies" that take place between members of Congress in which a member asks a bill's sponsors detailed questions about provisions of a bill, usually with the intention of getting an interpretation favorable to the questioner.

A spirited controversy has raged over the use of legislative histories as guides for judges. The attack on these histories has been led by Justice Antonin Scalia and a group of conservative jurists who are known, collectively, as "textualists." These legal scholars find three basic flaws in resorting to legislative histories to guide their interpretation. The first is that only the bill itself, not the elaborate supporting documentation of the legislative history, is what has been duly enacted by Congress. They say, "Look to the bare wording of the bill itself, not the committee report, or the floor debate." They also point out that it is highly unlikely that all members of Congress were participants throughout the entire process. Congress, after all, is a highly specialized institution in which a member of the Senate Finance Committee who is an expert on tax policy may know very little about defense policy and will probably have had little to do with participating in legislation related to the military. So what, indeed, is congressional intent, when only a tiny fraction of the membership of Congress has been involved?[6]

A second objection by the textualists is that the use of legislative history represents a kind of power grab by judges, since it grants them an unwarranted degree of discretion. A judge, it is argued, can pick and choose among the various components of a legislative history to find the parts that suit his own preference as to how the case should turn out. The judge may choose to ignore the minority views in a committee report and embrace only the position of the committee's majority.[7]

The third point of the textualist attack in essence puts lawmakers on notice that if they were more precise in drafting legislation, there would be no need for judges to poke around in the legislative histories.[8]

Scalia's objection to the use of legislative history is not universally accepted within the federal appellate system. Indeed, some respected appeals court judges reject Scalia's point of view because "it seems to profess a greater duty to an abstract conception of 'The Law' than to the legislature."[9] But others who see Scalia's objections as reasonable assert, "Because Congress votes on bills, not committee reports, or floor speeches, and because the president cannot veto legislative history, a court should not give the force of law to the mere thoughts of Congress, regardless of Congress's actual subjective intent."[10]

Scalia's belief that Congress might be induced to write legislation with greater precision if the vast amount of supporting material were ignored is probably unrealistic. Congress, for all its specialization, has never been able to produce laws whose meanings would be self-evident to every intelligent reader. Moreover, Congress has often been lazy and careless in drafting laws, believing that the bureaucrats who are charged with executing them will apply reasonable interpretations; frankly, they are sometimes happy to wash their hands of a complex or intractable problem.

The looseness of Congressional language may also result from the manner in which the House and Senate conduct their business. As Robert Katzmann points out:

> . . . [L]egislation is often ambiguous because the problems confronted are not simply defined and Congress lacks the expertise to solve them . . . sometimes it is too much to expect Congress to

foresee all manner of developments. In other circumstances . . . ambiguity is a deliberate strategy to secure a majority coalition in support of the legislation. In any case, exhorting the legislative branch to write unambiguous legislation will have little effect.[11]

Conflicts over statutory interpretation certainly contribute to tensions between Congress and Court but are a less serious irritant than determinations that acts of Congress are unconstitutional.

Pay, Perks, and Proprieties

The Constitution granted to Congress substantial authority over the federal judiciary. Immediately after ratification, as we saw in Chapter 1, Congress enacted the Judiciary Act of 1789, which, in addition to its famously unconstitutional Section 13, created a system of "inferior" courts, the US Courts of Appeals. The Constitution also gives to Congress the power to define the appellate jurisdiction of the Supreme Court. Congress, moreover, can impeach and remove federal judges, including justices of the Supreme Court, and it appropriates money for the operation of the federal courts, as it does with the departments of the executive branch. Of the thirteen annual appropriations bills, one is for the State Department, the Justice Department, and the Judiciary. The appropriations committee of each house of Congress has subcommittees that deal with the budgets of those three parts of the government.

With its ability to determine how much justices are paid and the areas on which the Supreme Court may hear appeals, Congress has a great deal to say about the quality of life and work in the federal courts. In addition, the two judiciary committees have the responsibility to oversee the federal courts and the manner in which the enactments of Congress are enforced. Accordingly, Congress oversees such things as the functioning of the criminal justice system at the federal level. The quality of oversight varies greatly in Congress. Some committees take the responsibility seriously, while others conduct oversight only in response to crises or scandals.

One notable oversight hearing by the House Judiciary Committee took place on June 11, 1998, under the chairmanship of Rep. Howard Coble, a North Carolina Republican. The witnesses represented an organization called the Judicial Conference of the United States, which was created in 1922 to serve as the principal policymaking body for the federal court system. Its membership consists of twenty-seven federal judges, headed by the Chief Justice of the United States. The Conference meets twice yearly. Among other things, these meetings make recommendations to Congress on legislation affecting the federal judiciary. It is, in effect, the liaison between the federal courts and Congress; it airs the grievances of the judges and receives the complaints of the members of Congress. It is the principal point of routine contact between the two branches.

Congressional complaints abounded that particular day. Among them were concerns about travel by federal judges paid for by the taxpayers or by private organizations. There was a hint that some of the privately financed travel was paid for by companies that had business before the federal courts. This concern intensified in May 2004, when Chief Justice William H. Rehnquist accepted the use of a corporate jet to fly him to Ohio to give a speech.[12]

A related complaint from the lawmakers was that federal judges were failing to ensure that they had no financial interest in companies who came before their courts. The grievances on the part of the judges consisted of the failure of Congress to increase the cost-of-living adjustment in judges' salaries. They also complained about overcrowded and antiquated courthouses.[13]

The pay issue was especially sensitive. Members of Congress tend to resist pay increases for federal judges that will result in the judges making more than they do. The Judicial Conference, accordingly, usually couches its appeal for higher pay for judges in a larger plea for higher salaries for members of Congress. Members of Congress, for their part, are sensitive to the fact that their $162,000 annual salary looks very big to the average voter. By placing their pay increases in the same appropriations package as cost-of-living adjustments for federal judges and civil servants, they get a certain amount of political cover.

Shortly after she announced her retirement from the Supreme Court in July 2005, Justice Sandra Day O'Connor expressed her concern about the tattered state of relations between Congress and the federal courts: "In all the years of my life," she said, "I've never seen relations as strained as they are now between the judiciary and some members of Congress. The present climate is such that I worry about the future of the federal judiciary. For one thing, Congress has not seen fit to have judicial salaries keep pace with what would be expected of people in equivalent professions."[14]

Encounters between congressional committees and the Judicial Conference can turn very nasty, as one did on March 16, 2004, when Rep. James Sensenbrenner, a Wisconsin Republican and chairman of the House Judiciary Committee, spoke. Sensenbrenner, known for his acerbic manner, began by launching an attack on the chief judge of the US District Court of Minnesota for departing from the federal sentencing guidelines enacted by Congress and handing out a more lenient sentence to an offender. When Sensenbrenner demanded court records to see if these departures were part of a larger pattern, he was denied the data he sought.[15]

He then went after Judge Richard D. Cudahy of the 7th Circuit Court of Appeals for leaking confidential grand jury material to a journalist. When Sensenbrenner complained about this to the chief judge of the 7th Circuit, Richard Posner, the chief judge, in Sensenbrenner's words, "simply whitewashed the matter regarding his colleague Judge Cudahy *without conducting any investigation*" (emphasis in the original). Sensenbrener's parting shot was a harsh criticism of the Supreme Court for citing foreign laws and judicial proceedings in the interpretation of the US Constitution.[16]

In response to the criticism of Sensenbrenner, Chief Justice Rehnquist created a committee consisting of six federal judges to investigate the handling of judicial misconduct. Unlike members of Congress, who are held accountable through elections, federal judges with lifetime tenure are shielded from most public scrutiny. Some legal scholars saw in the creation of the committee the possibility of greater judicial accountability.[17]

The financial plight of judges, their unwillingness to disclose financial connections to litigants who come before their court, the failure by Congress to provide money to alleviate crowding in courthouses, a leak to a reporter by a judge, or even a jurist's departure from sentencing guidelines enacted by Congress may seem rather inconsequential points of conflict between the legislative and judicial branches. In the aggregate, however, they provide a picture of mutual wariness, suspicion, jealousy, and even a bit of spite. How petty they all seem when judged against the majesty of the basic framework of the Constitution and the grand design of the separation of powers. But there are other zones of tension that rise to a higher level of constitutional consequence and come very near to defining the differences between Congress and the federal courts, and the US Supreme Court in particular. Conflicts over pay and working conditions are probably a symptom of tensions between the legislative and judicial branches rather than a cause.

Don't Make a Federal Case Out of It!

An especially sore point of contention between the federal courts and Congress is the practice of Congress of raising to the federal level problems that have traditionally been viewed as within the jurisdiction of the states.

In 1998, the American Bar Association convened a task force on "The Federalization of Criminal Law." The seventeen-member panel, consisting of distinguished lawyers from academia, private practice, and government service, wasted no time in identifying the problem. They were told "by more than one source that many of these new federal laws are passed not because federal prosecution of these crimes is necessary but because federal crime legislation in general is thought to be politically popular. Put another way, it is not considered politically wise to vote [in Congress] against crime legislation, even if it is misguided, unnecessary, and even harmful."[18]

The trend toward making every notorious crime a federal offense is a recent phenomenon. As the report stated, "More than 40 percent of the federal criminal provisions enacted since the Civil War have been enacted since 1970." Moreover, "All signs indicate that the federalization trend is growing, not slowing . . . an estimated 1,000 bills dealing with criminal statutes were introduced in the most recent Congress."[19]

What accounted for this dramatic rise in Congress commandeering criminal law, traditionally a state and local responsibility under the police powers reserved to the states by the Constitution? A novel theory of federalism, perhaps? The task force answered the question bluntly: "Writer after writer has noticed the absence of any underlying principle governing Congressional choice to criminalize conduct under federal law that is already criminalized by state law."[20]

While the task force could not identify an underlying principle, they did identify a cause: "Particularly notorious conduct receiving widespread media attention frequently prompts Congressional criminalization [that gains] popularity among constituents."[21]

The federalization of criminal law, from the perspective of the federal judges, is part of a larger problem of increasingly heavy caseloads. Paul Light cites an example of legislation that would have enabled veterans to appeal to the federal courts when they had been denied benefits. During negotiations on the bill in Congress, a compromise was put forward to enable veterans to appeal their cases to specialized courts set up for the sole purpose of hearing veterans' appeals or to the regular federal court system. Federal judges became so alarmed about the possibility that their already heavy caseloads would increase that they took the unusual step of lobbying Congress to create the specialized courts. Light adds the following observation: "There is a profound lack of comity between Congress and the judicial branch. Neither understands the other well. The lack of underlying appreciation for the political workload pressures in each branch often comes to the fore when one branch needs something from the other."[22]

Free Exercise and "Position-Taking"

Three decades ago, David R. Mayhew identified several activities by which members of Congress can improve their reelection prospects. One of these he called "position-taking," which he defined as "the public enunciation of a judgmental statement on anything likely to be of interest to political actors. The statement may take the form of a roll call vote."[23]

Roll call votes are recorded votes that formally register a member or senator in favor of or opposed to a bill or amendment. A speech designed to ingratiate the member with his or her constituency may do just as well, but a roll call vote puts a member of Congress on the public record.

Free exercise of religion lends itself especially well to position-taking, since few would argue with the desirability of the freest possible exercise of religion. Survey data has always reported exceedingly high percentages of Americans who consider themselves religious. A *Newsweek*/Beliefnet poll taken in August 2005, for example, indicated that more than half of all respondents (55 percent) considered spirituality very important in their daily lives and an additional 27 percent deemed it "somewhat important."[24] It would seem likely that this popular majority would strenuously oppose limitations on religious institutions or individuals practicing their faith.

Interest groups representing various religions enjoy considerable public support and a high degree of moral prestige, and as Mayhew has observed, Congress is especially good at "servicing the organized," being responsive to interest groups with memberships broad enough to have significant numbers of affiliated voters in every state and most congressional districts.[25] "At voicing opinions held by significant numbers of voters back in the constituencies, the United States Congress is extraordinarily effective."[26]

As we have seen in the responses to the *Goldman* decision and the reactions to *Smith* and *Boerne*, the religious community has been unanimous in support of the most generous interpretation of the meaning of free exercise and of the restoration of the strictest barriers to government limitations on such exercise. It would take a bold senator or House member to oppose what amounts to a consensus across both the religious spectrum and the political spectrum. Free exercise is not just a popular issue; it stands at the very summit of public approval, and its supporting constituency of interest groups is vigilant, highly motivated, and able to speak with moral authority.

A Constitutionally Casual Congress?

Since its members face periodic reelection, Congress is an institution that must on some level be responsive to the needs and demands of voters and interest groups. The response may not be the immediate enactment of a law, but if the clamor represents more than just a few isolated pleas for action, members of the House and Senate will not ignore them, even if the response is nothing more than rhetorical position-taking.

But if the demands are more sustained and seem to reflect an extensive body of opinion expressed broadly in everything from calls and e-mails to editorials and visits, some response is usually forthcoming. If the solution is not unduly complicated and does not involve the establishment or restructuring of a major federal program, there will be a effort to fix it quickly. "Quickly" is of course a relative term when applied to Congress. As Louis Froman observed more than three decades ago:

> [The] legislative process is . . . lengthy and time-consuming with many opportunities for delay. A major reason for is that the relatively autonomous committees often consist of members with different kinds of constituents. This usually produces built-in conflict in each unit. . . . [The] speed with which legislation passes the House or Senate is in large measure determined by the nature of the conflict. . . .[27]

The legislation enacted by Congress in the aftermath of the *Smith* decision involved only nominal conflict and no jurisdictional disputes among committees. In addition, David Mayhew's observation about Congress's readiness to service well-organized groups applies with particular relevance to religious organizations on issues that affect them. On free exercise questions, religious groups are uniquely equipped to move swiftly, and Congress is especially responsive. As Louis Fisher observed: "With ready access to parishioners, religious interests can mobilize more quickly and effectively than nearly any other interest group. As a result, legislatures—supposedly rough institutions designed to satisfy the majority's interests—have shown a keen sensitivity and solicitude in protecting minority rights. For this reason, on matters of religious faith and observance, elected officials played an integral role in defining the reaches of religious liberty protections."[28]

The Religious Freedom Restoration Act was introduced by Rep. Solarz on July 26, 1990, nine days after the *Smith v. Employment Division* decision was handed down. It was signed by President Clinton on November 16, 1993, three years and five months after introduction. On the face of it, this may not appear to be an especially speedy enactment, but it is important to bear in mind that the introduction of the bill came just a few days before the August recess, when members of Congress return home to campaign for the fall elections. In that election, the bill's sponsor and most energetic advocate, Rep. Solarz, was defeated for reasons totally unrelated to his sponsorship of RFRA. Such conflict as emerged in the Senate hearings in 1993 was over the need for right-to-life advocates to be assured that RFRA did not establish abortion as a free exercise right, an interpretation that most of the bill's backers considered improbable. When that issue was clarified, the bill rolled smoothly on to passage.

The issue of the constitutionality of the bill was raised by just one witness, Bruce Fein, the conservative legal scholar who had served as deputy attorney general in the Reagan administration.

He based his objection to RFRA on the grounds that it violated the principle of federalism. The argument appeared to have little influence on the members of Congress.

Likewise, after the *Boerne* decision in 1997, congressional response was quick. Again, however, an August recess intervened, and it was not until 1998 that RLPA, the Religious Liberty Protection Act, was introduced in the House. In the Senate, it was February 2000 before Senator Hatch introduced the companion bill, which ran into immediate trouble from Senator Kennedy, who raised many of the same objections to the bill that Rep. Nadler and others had raised in the House. Nonetheless, under its new name, the Religious Land Use and Institutionalized Persons Act, Kennedy's concerns were allayed, no new hearings were held, the hearing record was simply borrowed from RLPA, and by September the bill had been passed unanimously in both houses and signed into law by President Clinton. By the leisurely standards of Congress, the enactment of this legislation was almost brisk.

In light of the Supreme Court's decision in *Smith*, the Oregon peyote case, it would have seemed natural for Congress to be deeply concerned about questions of constitutionality. Recall that Douglas Laycock had testified before Rep. Canady's subcommittee that any attempt simply to resurrect RFRA would likely be held unconstitutional, and that Congress had to tread a narrow path. The use of Section 5 powers to restore the *Sherbert* standard had been treated by the Supreme Court as a usurpation by Congress of the Court's power to interpret the Constitution, and the use of the Commerce Clause had been significantly constricted by the *Lopez* case involving the Gun-Free Schools Act. Nonetheless, in the process of writing RLPA and then substituting RLUIPA, questions of constitutionality did not loom large in the discussions.

A picture emerges, then, of a Congress that is "constitutionally casual." This tendency is especially notable when legislation enjoys widespread popularity and is supported by powerful interest groups that are viewed favorably by the public—for example, veterans, firefighters, or handicapped children. Free exercise of religion would be at the top of any list of popular causes. Who, after all, would feel comfortable opposing legislation entitled the "Religious Freedom Restoration Act"?

Why would Congress be so casual about the constitutional implications of popular bills, when an unfavorable ruling by the Supreme Court would force them to go back to square one and start the entire legislative process all over again? One reason, as we have seen, is that Congress is never compelled to completely reinvent legislation. When RLPA failed to pass, it was quickly altered and renamed. The hearings of RLPA were simply grafted on to RLUIPA.

Congress is not totally inattentive to questions of constitutionality, but a recent study by J. Mitchell Pickerell raises important questions about whether doubts about the constitutionality of legislation would influence members of Congress to vote against it, especially if it was popular. His survey of members, former members, congressional staff, and lobbyists revealed that they, "did not believe that constitutionality was an important consideration in Congress when legislation was drafted and considered."[29] There is abundant evidence from the hearings and debates on free exercise legislation that members of Congress are aware of the possible unconstitutionality of bills they are considering, but qualms on the part of members of Congress about a bill's constitutionality recede if there is a popular groundswell in favor of it. There is a payoff for members of Congress as individuals for being associated, even in a losing cause, with a popular bill. And, from the perspective of good public policy, many members of Congress seem to feel that "no harm has been done" when a popular bill fails the test of constitutionality.

Senator Patrick Leahy, the Vermont Democrat who once found himself alone in opposition to the Communications Decency Act because he considered it an unconstitutional abridgement of the freedom of speech, put it this way: A lot of people can vote for something popular and say, "Well, if it's unconstitutional that's what the Supreme Court is for. And how do we know—

they might rule it constitutional. So why should senators worry about it, that's the Court's job."[30]

For a popularly elected body, winning favor with voters is essential if one wishes to be reelected. For their part, judges would not wish to show contempt for the popular will, but their situation is quite distinct from that of legislators. They are well aware that legislators who need to face the voters are in a far different and more vulnerable situation than those on the federal bench.

We need go no further to demonstrate this than a speech given by Associate Justice John Paul Stevens to a group of lawyers in Las Vegas, Nevada, in the late summer of 2005. Stevens used the occasion to review a number of decisions that had been handed down recently by the Supreme Court. Justice Stevens confessed early in his speech that in each of the decisions, "I was convinced that the law compelled a result that I would have opposed if I were a legislator."[31]

Directly and with considerable candor, Stevens pointed to the most salient difference between a Supreme Court justice and a member of Congress:

> While the desire for popularity is a matter that poses a threat to the independence of every elected judge, thanks to the foresight of men like Alexander Hamilton who provided us with lifetime tenure, our job is vastly simplified by our duty to allow legislatures and executives to fashion policy in response to their understanding of the popular will.[32]

Supreme Court justices are not sealed off in a doctrinal bell jar and are not wholly unresponsive to the popular mood. When they go home at night, they watch the same news programs and read the same newspapers as members of Congress. Moreover, in the Washington community, Supreme Court justices and members of Congress are part of the same social circle and encounter one another in a variety of nonofficial settings. It is true, however, that the Court's focus is less what the public thinks or even what Congress thinks, but rather on constitutional ground rules of which the public is generally unaware and about which Congress can sometimes be remarkably casual:

> The Supreme Court is not indifferent to what Congress thinks of it. . . . [J]ustices might try to calculate whether their preferred interpretation of a statute would make enough members of Congress sufficiently unhappy to produce . . . an override. If so, the justices would modify their interpretations to avoid such a result. . . . It may be, however, that most justices do not care that much whether Congress overrides their decisions, except on issues that are especially important to them.[33]

This foregoing statement refers, of course, to the Supreme Court's responsibility for statutory interpretation, but it also applies to constitutional interpretation, as we saw in the case of Simcha Goldman, the air force psychologist. In that case, the justices did not attempt to challenge an act of Congress that nullified a previous Supreme Court ruling upholding the military's dress code. But the Court is assertive when it feels that Congress has intruded on its turf. There is no better example of the turf-consciousness of the Court than its decision in the *Boerne* case that Congress had exceeded its authority under Section 5 of the Fourteenth Amendment and had, in fact, usurped the power of the Supreme Court to interpret the Constitution. Such an intrusion was very important to a majority of the justices. It was viewed as a challenge not only to the institution, but to the justices as individuals. As James Madison noted in *Federalist* 51, "The interest of the man must be connected with the constitutional rights of the place." The effectiveness of separation of powers is reinforced by the fact that in American politics, it is difficult to separate the institutional from the personal.

Nonetheless, politics is the context in which Congress and the Supreme Court conduct their business, and it shapes their views on such important issues as free exercise of religion far more than personality differences or even contrasting views of their role in the federal system. Put succinctly by former law professor and current Columbia University president Lee C. Bollinger, "Everybody knows there's a difference between acting within a body of jurisprudence and acting politically."[34]

Who Better Protects Our Rights, Congress or the Courts?

After reading this book, the reader might well conclude that, at least in recent years, the Congress of the United States is a far more vigorous defender of the rights of free exercise than the Supreme Court. As Louis Fisher has noted, "The Supreme Court has competed with nonjudicial institutions for two hundred years, sometimes leading the charge for minority rights, but more often pulling up the rear. . . . A review of Supreme Court holdings reveals some victories for religious minorities and many, many defeats."[35]

We have certainly seen numerous instances of government invasions of the free exercise rights of minorities—the Mormons, the Amish, *Santería* churches, Orthodox Jews, and Native Americans. But American religious groups, as we have seen, are not powerless, especially in light of the ability of these groups to form mighty coalitions that create irresistible pressure on Congress. More than ninety religious groups banded together in 1999 to demand that Congress pass the Religious Liberty Protection Act, a law to reverse the decision in the *Boerne* case—hardly a persecuted minority.

When aroused, the passion of religious groups often overwhelms opposition. Even the objection of the military, perhaps the most respected institution in America, was insufficient to withstand the force of the opposition of religious groups to the air force's attempt to ban religious headgear in the interest of good order and discipline.

Matters relating to the free exercise of religion are in a class by themselves because of the singular role played by religion in American life. Which institution—the Congress or the Supreme Court—is best equipped to determine what is in the public interest when conflicts arise between a church wishing to increase the size of its sanctuary to accommodate a growing congregation and a town seeking to preserve its historic character? Are life-tenured judges or members of Congress, who must face the voters, better at finding a decent compromise between a state that is trying to limit the use of drugs and a religious group for whom the use of peyote is central to its worship? Surprisingly, the attorney who argued successfully on behalf of the City of Boerne and convinced the Supreme Court to overturn the Religious Freedom Restoration Act argues that it is Congress.[36] But when religious disputes arise in the congressional environment, the give-and-take of compromise that mitigates conflict in other areas of policy gives way to the kind of posturing and bluster that we saw in the Terri Schiavo case. As law professor William E. Nelson concludes in his recent book, *Marbury v. Madison*:

> Americans . . . agree that racial, religious, and comparable forms of discrimination are profoundly evil and unjust. They also seem to understand that legislatures chosen through majoritarian, democratic processes sometimes lack the impartiality to provide the necessary protection that victims of discrimination deserve. Only judges are sufficiently insulated from majority prejudices to be trusted.[37]

The Terri Schiavo case may be an exception that does not cast doubt on the ability of elected legislatures to protect constitutional rights in an orderly and responsible manner. To concede that the Congress is incapable of acting responsibly is to give up on a principal element of popular government. As Alan Wolfe has warned those who turn routinely to the courts for the vindication of minority rights; ". . . [I]t is a mistake to rely on the courts to make policy, as the fine art of convincing voters through the democratic process of the validity of their beliefs is lost."[38]

The search for the single consistent and dependable champion of individual rights among the institutions of American government produces no clear winner. We can only hope that in the space between the judicial detachment of the courts and the democratic legitimacy of the elected branches none of our rights will fall undetected and unprotected.

Notes

1. Robert A. Katzmann, *Courts and Congress* (Washington DC: The Brookings Institution, 1997), 16.
2. Michael O'Brien, *Philip Hart, Conscience of the Senate* (East Lansing, MI: Michigan State University Press, 1995), 122.
3. Roger H. Davidson, "What Judges Ought To Know About Lawmaking in Congress," in Robert A. Katzmann, ed., *Judges and Legislators* (Washington DC: The Brookings Institution, 1988), 93.
4. Ibid., 95.
5. James Q. Wilson, ed., *The Politics of Regulation* (New York: Basic Books, 1980), 390.
6. Katzmann, *Courts and Congress*, 58.
7. Ibid.
8. Ibid.
9. "Why Learned Hand Would Never Consult Legislative History," 105 Harv. L. Rev. 1005, p. 1.
10. Ibid., 2.
11. Katzmann, *Courts and Congress*, 61.
12. Michael Janofsky, "Ohio Groups Question Justice's Trip on Utility Jet," *New York Times*, May 15, 2004.
13. US Congress, House, Hearing Before the Subcommittee on Courts of the Committee on the Judiciary of The United States Judicial Conference, Administrative Office and Federal Judicial Center and the "Protecting American Small Business Trade Act of 1998, 105th Congress, 2nd sess., June 11, 1978.
14. Sarah Kershaw, "O'Connor Sees Strains between Judiciary and Some in Congress," *New York Times*, July 22, 2005.
15. US House of Representatives News Advisory "Sensenbrenner Remarks before the U.S. Judicial Conference Regarding Congressional Oversight Responsibility of the Judiciary," March 16, 2004. www.house .gov/judiciary/news031604.htm
16. Ibid.
17. Mike Allen and Brian Faler, "Judicial Discipline to Be Examined," *The Washington Post*, May 26, 2004.
18. American Bar Association, Criminal Justice Section, *The Federalization of Criminal Law* (Washington DC: American Bar Association, 1998), 2.
19. Ibid., 11.
20. Ibid., 15.
21. Ibid.
22. Paul C. Light, *Forging Legislation* (New York: W. W. Norton & Company, 1992), 177.

23. David R. Mayhew, *Congress: The Electoral Connection* (New Haven, CT: Yale University Press, 1974), 61.
24. www.beliefnet.com/story/173
25. Mayhew, *Congress*, 130.
26. Ibid., 106.
27. Lewis A. Froman, Jr., *The Congressional Process* (Boston: Little, Brown and Company, 1967), 17.
28. Louis Fisher, "Nonjudicial Safeguards for Religious Liberty," *University of Cincinnati Law Review* 70: 96.
29. J. Mitchell Pickerell, *Constitutional Deliberation in Congress* (Durham, NC: Duke University Press, 2004), 134.
30. Telephone interview with Senator Patrick Leahy, September 30, 2005.
31. Address to the Clark County Bar Association Luncheon Meeting, Thursday, August 18, 2005, Wynn Hotel, Las Vegas, Nevada.
32. Ibid.
33. Laurence Baum, *The Supreme Court*, 7th ed. (Washington DC: CQ Press, 2001), 176.
34. John W. Broder, "Have a Seat, Your Honor (Presidents Wish It Were That Easy)," *The New York Times*, July 10, 2005.
35. Pickerell, *Constitutional Deliberation*, 95.
36. Marci A. Hamilton, *God vs. the Gavel* (New York: Cambridge University Press, 2005), 303.
37. William E. Nelson, *Marbury v. Madison, the Origins and Legacy of Judicial Review* (Lawrence, KS: University of Kansas Press, 2000), 124.
38. Alan Wolfe, "The Culture Wars," *The Responsive Community* 14 (Spring/Summer 2004): 38.

Index